HYPERMODERN
CHESS

(formerly titled "Nimzovich The Hypermodern")

dover publications inc. new york n. y.

HYPERMODERN CHESS:

AS DEVELOPED IN THE GAMES OF ITS GREATEST EXPONENT, **ARON NIMZOVICH.** THE DEFINITE COLLECTION OF NIMZOVICH'S REVOLU- TIONARY GAMES AND THEIR STARTLING UNCONVENTIONAL THEORIES, EDITED BY FRED REINFELD

Manufactured in United States of America

contents

NO OTHER master's games are so rich in human interest and dramatic appeal as are those of Aron Nimzovich. Perhaps this is due to the fact that he not only had to win his games against his opponents, but in addition he had to win over a hostile chess world. At every one of his games there was a specter, an unseen enemy. It added a cruel burden to the crushing tasks which tournament play imposes under the best of conditions.

I do not propose to repeat my description of Nimzovich's career which appeared in a recent volume.* In the present work, such a description would be doubly superfluous, as the games speak eloquently for themselves. Arranged chronologically, they demonstrate in a very exciting way why Nimzovich became one of the most famous and most eagerly imitated masters.

Because the planning of this work required that the games should have this graphic quality, a great deal of thought went into their selection. I frankly aimed at a "popular." book, one which could be relished by all chessplayers, regardless of their playing ability. I avoided over-long games, which (let it be confessed for once!) tend to bore the reader. I wanted relatively short, sharp, witty encounters which make their point in an unforgettably drastic manner. I attempted to give as many games as possible which have not appeared in *My System*. Yet where the merit of the games was so outstanding that duplication was unavoidable, I sought to vary the notes; to adopt a different standpoint, to

* Nimzovich: *My System*. Edited by Fred Reinfeld. David McKay Company. Philadelphia, 1947.

make the comments fuller, to adapt them to the needs of the average chessplayer.

These are games which do not yield up all their subtlety and savor on the first examination. They bear re-playing. The reader will always find new facets in them. I was familiar with Nimzovich's theories and with some of his masterpieces long before *My System* was published in English; and today I can look back over almost a quarter of a century of absorbed study and keen enjoyment of Nimzovich's games. There are some which I must have played over at least twenty times. Yet their magic still lives on, and with every re-playing, some new fine point comes to light. If some of the pleasure is communicated to the reader by this book, I shall feel well repaid.

New York,   FRED REINFELD
August 22, 1947

HYPERMODERN
CHESS

1. *"The Child is Father of the Man"*

IN THIS, the earliest known game of Nimzovich, we see three notable features of his later games: a surprising sacrifice in an apparently blocked position, delightfully subtle play with the Knights, and brilliant exploitation of a passed Pawn.

VIENNA GAME

Coburg, 1904
("B" Tournament)

WHITE: *A. Nimzovich*   BLACK: *W. Hilse*

1	P—K4	P—K4
2	Kt—QB3	Kt—QB3
3	B—B4	B—B4
4	P—Q3	

In this rather romantic opening, which Nimzovich never adopted in his mature period, 4 Q—Kt4 is a good alternative; if then 4 . . . Q—B3; 5 Kt—Q5! with a powerful attack.

4	. . . .	P—Q3
5	P—B4	Kt—B3
6	P—B5	P—KR3

To prevent the annoying pin B—KKt5; but the text creates a target for a Pawn-storming advance by White. Mieses specialized in this procedure.

7	P—KKt4	Kt—QR4
8	Q—B3	Kt × B
9	P × Kt	P—B3
10	B—Q2	P—R3
11	O—O—O	P—QKt4

Both sides play sharply for attack.

12	KKt—K2	B—Kt2
13	P—KR4	Q—K2
14	P—Kt5	Kt—Q2
15	Kt—Kt3	P—B3

Nimzovich has offered his Pawn at QB4 because he has no good way to guard it, and he does not care to play BP × P, which opens an attacking file for Black. His opponent, on the other hand, sees no tangible gain from capturing the Pawn—although he changes his mind next move.

16 B—K3 *!*   KtP × P

Black's best course is 16 . . . O—O—O, getting his King to a reasonably safe place and connecting his Rooks. The text is risky, and the same would be true of 16 . . . RP × P; 17 RP × P, R × R (better 17 . . . O—O—O); 18 R × R, B × B *ch;* 19 Q × B, BP × P; 20 R—R5 etc.

17 Q—R5 *ch !*   K—Q1

Relatively better is 17 . . . Q—B2; 18 Q × Q *ch,* K × Q; 19 B × B, Kt × B; 20 R × P, RP × P etc. After the text, Black's game becomes difficult because his King is insecure.

18 B × B   Kt × B
19 Q—K2   K—K1

. . . K—B2 at once saves time. If, however, 19 . . . BP × P; 20 P—B6 *!,* Q × P; 21 KR—B1 with a winning attack.

20 P × BP   P × P
21 Q × P   P—QR4

Threatening . . . B—R3.

22 Q—K2   K—Q2
23 R—R2   QR—KKt1
24 Q—K3   K—B2

Black has finally provided for his King and brought out his Queen's Rook—but at considerable cost of wasted time.

25 R(2)—Q2   R—Q1
26 Kt—R5   Q—B2
27 Kt—Kt3   P—R4
28 R—Kt2   QR—KKt1 *?*

The other Rook should have played here; but Nimzovich's startling reply was not easy to foresee.

29 R × P *! !*   K × R

Schlechter points out that if 29 . . . R × Kt; 30 Q × Kt,

R × R; 31 Kt—Kt5 *ch*, K—B1
(or 31 . . . K—Kt1; 32 Q—
R7 *ch*, K—B1; 33 R × P *ch*);
32 R × P *ch !*, B × R; 33 Kt—
Q6 *ch* wins!

30 R—Q2 *ch*   K—B2

If 30 . . . K—K2; 31 Q ×
Kt *ch*, K—K1; 32 Kt(Kt3)—
K2 and the threat of 33 R—Q6
gives White a winning position.

31 Q × Kt   K—Kt1

Here is the final point of the
combination: If 31 . . . R ×
Kt; 32 Kt—Kt5 *ch* leads to the
win of Black's Queen! A
Nimzovich finesse!

32 Q—Q6 *ch*   K—R1
33 Kt(Kt3)—K2   R—Q1
34 Q—B5   R × R
35 Q × P *ch*   K—Kt1
36 K × R   Q—Q2 *ch*
37 K—B1   R—Q1

The upshot of Nimzovich's
combination is that he has two
Pawns for the exchange, plus
lasting pressure on Black's exposed King.

38 P—Kt4   Q—QB2
39 Q—B5   R—Kt1
40 P—R4   Q—Q1 ?

Black plays this phase weakly. He should either place his
Rook in the vicinity of his
King, or else try . . . R—Kt5,
so as to create a formidable
counterchance in the shape of
a passed Rook Pawn. Such positions call for fighting chess.

41 P—Kt5   P × P
42 Q × P   K—R1
43 Q—B5   R—Kt2 ?

43 . . . R—Kt5 forces White
to take a draw with 44 Kt—
Kt5, K—Kt1; 45 Q—R7 *ch*,
K—B1; 46 Q—B5 *ch*, K—Kt1;
47 Q—R7 *ch* etc.

44 K—Kt2   K—Kt1
45 Kt—B1   R—QB2
46 Q—Kt5   K—B1
47 Kt—Kt3   Q—Q2
48 Q—K2   Q—B2
49 Kt—Kt5   R—Q2
50 Kt—B5   R—Q1

Black has given his opponent
time to post the Knights in-
vincibly. He soon pays the pen-
alty.

51 Kt—K6   R—Q2
52 Q—B4 *ch*   K—Kt1
53 Kt—B5 *! !*

60	Kt × BP	R × P
61	Kt × RP	

An astonishing position! If 53 . . . Q × Q; 54 Kt × R *ch*, followed by 55 Kt—Kt6 *ch* in reply to a King move.

53	R—K2
54 Q × Q	R × Q
55 Kt—Q6	R—Kt2
56 Kt(5) × B	R—Kt5

The only chance . . . such as it is. 56 . . . R × Kt *ch*; 57 Kt × R, K × Kt is hopeless.

57 Kt—B5 !	R × RP
58 Kt—Q3 !	R—Kt5
59 Kt—K8 !	

The Knight moves are all part of a forced win. Now that the Rook is cut off from KB5, White's King Bishop Pawn will march in.

59	R × P

61 . . . .   P—K5

Equally delightful is 61 . . . R—Kt5; 62 Kt × P, R—Kt4; 63 Kt—Kt7 *!*, R × Kt (. . . R × P is not good enough, as White still has one Pawn for mating purposes!); 64 P—B6, R—Kt2 *ch;* 65 K—B1 and wins: the Rook must be given up for the advanced Pawn.

62 P—B6 !	R—R4
63 P—B7	R—KB4
64 Kt—K5 !	P—K6

If 64 . . . K—B1; 65 Kt—Kt7, R—B3; 66 Kt—K6 *!*

65 Kt—Kt3 *!*   Resigns

A delicious ending.

2. The Old Order Changeth

IN ANY given period, the chess world is ruled by outstanding masters in their prime who are so famous that it is difficult to imagine their ever being dethroned. Yet, as old age creeps up on the reigning players, new names and new faces appear and create sensations by their revolutionary victories against the ruling hierarchy.

Thus it was during the first decade of this century, when the Age of Tarrasch was coming to an end. For some fifteen years the theories of Tarrasch had governed master chess. Suddenly new, fresh powers began to appear on the scene. Two of the most important newcomers were Nimzovich and Spielmann. Like a refreshing breeze their bright games swept away the stale air of the deadening technique of Tarrasch.

FALKBEER COUNTER GAMBIT

Match, 1906

WHITE: *R. Spielmann*   BLACK: *A. Nimzovich*

1 P—K4	P—K4
2 P—KB4	P—Q4
3 KP × P	P—QB3 *! ?*

Nimzovich must be quite eager to snatch the attack from his opponent. The best reply is probably 4 Kt—QB3, BP × ·P; 5 P × P, P—Q5; 6 Kt—K4, Q—Q4; 7 B—Q3 *!*, Kt—QB3; 8 Q—K2 with advantage for

White (Euwe).

4 Q—B3

This turns out badly.
(*See diagram on next page*)

4 . . . .   KP × P

More in the spirit of this line of play is the two-Pawn sacrifice for development: 4 . . .

P—K5 *!?*; 5 Q × P *ch*, B—K2;
6 P × P, Kt × P followed by
. . . Kt—B3 and . . . O—O.

5 P × P

And now 5 P—Q4 gives
White better prospects of completing his development in a
rational manner.

5 . . . .   Kt × P
6 B—Kt5

Here Janowski recommends
6 P—B3 followed by 7 P—Q4.
The opening play is certainly
erratic!

6 . . . .   Kt—B3 *!*

Tempting White to lose valuable time with 7 B × Kt *ch*,
P × B; 8 Q × P *ch*, B—Q2
etc.

7 P—Q4   B—Q2
8 Kt—K2   Q—Kt3 *!*

Just at the right moment:
White's King Bishop and
Queen Pawn are menaced, and
9 B × Kt, B × B is obviously
in Black's favor.

9 Q—Q3   B—Q3
10 P—B4 ?

Loosening up his Pawn po-
sition for the sake of playing to
win a piece. 10 O—O was
safer.

10 . . . .   O—O *!*

He accepts the challenge.

11 B × Kt

The immediate 11 P—B5 is
effectively answered by 11

. . . Q—R4 *ch;* 12 B—Q2, Kt
—QKt5.

| 11 . . . . | B × B *!* |
| 12 P—B5 | |

White braves the attack, for
after 12 O—O, QR—Q1 he
would have a poor game.

12	B × BP
13 P × B	Q × BP
14 B × P	KR—K1

Despite his material advantage, White has a lost game:
his opponent's pieces are
posted too powerfully. The immediate threat is 15 . . . B—
Kt4.

| 15 Kt—B3 | B × P |
| 16 O—O—O | |

White gives up hope too
readily: He should have tried
16 KR—B1 (16 KR—Kt1 *??,*
Q × R *ch*), QR—Q1; 17 Q—
Kt5, Q × Q; 18 Kt × Q, B ×
R; 19 K × B and while White
is completely on the defensive,
he can put up a stubborn fight.
A likely continuation would
be: 19 . . . Kt—R4 *!;* 20 B—
B1 (if 20 B—Kt3, R—Q7 is
very strong), R—Q8 *ch;* 21 K

—B2, R—R8; 22 K—Kt2, R—
K8; 23 Kt(2)—B3, Kt—B5
ch; 24 B × Kt (else 24 . . .
Kt—Q6), R × R etc.

16	B × R
17 R × B	QR—Q1
18 Q—B2	

Although Black's forces have
come into action too strongly,
18 Q—B3 might have offered
somewhat better resistance.

| 18 . . . . | Kt—Q4 *!* |

19 B—Q2

If 19 Kt × Kt, Q × Q *ch;*
20 K × Q, R × Kt *ch;* 21 K—
Q3, R—K2; 22 K—B4, R—
K5 *ch;* 23 K—Q3, P—B4 and
wins (Janowski). After the
text, Black winds up neatly.

[9

| 19 . . . . | Kt—Kt5 ! | 21 K—Kt1 | Kt—B7 |

20 Q—Q1

Or 20 Q—Kt1, R × Kt etc.

20 . . . .   Kt—Q6 ch

White resigns. The ingenious Knight play is characteristic of Nimzovich's games.

3. Deus Ex Machina

EVEN as an inexperienced youngster, Nimzovich had the ability, in common with such masters as Lasker, Duras and Reshevsky, of discovering a diabolical resource in apparently hopeless positions. It was this ability which led the mature Nimzovich to include "the heroic defense" in his system. Tartakover's ironic aphorism "No one has yet managed to win a game by resigning" sums up the matter.

FRENCH DEFENSE

Zurich, 1906

WHITE: *A. Nimzovich*   BLACK: *Dr. G. Fluess*

1 P—K4	P—K3
2 P—Q4	P—Q4
3 Kt—QB3	

Later on Nimzovich was to proclaim the value of 3 P—K5 as a sovereign remedy against this defense.

3	Kt—KB3
4 B—Kt5	B—Kt5
5 P × P	

This gives Black no trouble at all. White can either strive violently for the initiative with 5 P—K5 or else play for a minimal advantage with 5 Kt —K2.

| 5 . . . . | Q × P |
| 6 B × Kt | B × Kt ch |

In later years, a good alternative was found in 6 . . .

P × B; 7 Q—Q2, Q—QR4 etc.
Black has an easy game.

7 P × B   P × B
8 Kt—B3   Kt—B3
9 B—K2

Leads to trouble. As he intends King-side castling, he
can obtain a much more secure
position with 9 P—Kt3 followed by 10 B—Kt2, which
incidentally saves time and
gives the Bishop a far more
active post.

9 . . . .   KR—Kt1
10 O—O ! ?

"Castling into it!"

10 . . . .   B—Q2
11 P—B4

He seeks to disengage
Black's attention from the
King-side, but only drives the
Queen to a more aggressive
spot.

11 . . . .   Q—KR4
12 P—Q5   O—O—O !

(See diagram in next column)

Now Nimzovich has an op-
portunity to achieve negative

immortality with 13 P × Kt ?,
B × P; 14 Q—B1, R × P ch!;
15 K × R(or 15 K—R1, R ×
P ch), R—Kt1 ch etc.

13 Kt—Q4 !

This deprives his King of an
important defending piece.
But it is part of a fiendish plan.
Most players would consider
White's game hopeless.

13 . . . .   Q—R6

One can hardly blame Black
for thinking that he has victory
within his grasp, but 13 . . .
Q—Kt4; 14 B—B3, Kt—K4
was a better course.

14 P—Kt3   R—Kt3

With the brutal threat 15
. . . R—R3. White seems lost.

[11

15 P × Kt ! !   B × P

Lasker dismisses the more tenacious 15 . . . R—R3 with an interesting refutation: 16 P × P ch ! (not 16 P × B ch, R × P; 17 B—R5, R × B; 18 R—K1, Q × RP ch; 19 K—B1, Q—R8 ch; 20 K—K2, Q—K5 ch and wins), K—Kt1 (if 16 . . . K × P; 17 B—B3 ch and White beats off the attack); 17 Kt—B6 ch, K × P; 18 Kt × R ch, K—B1; 19 Q × B ch, K × Q; 20 KR—Q1 ch followed by B—B3 and White's material advantage should prove decisive.

16 Kt × B !

But not 16 B—B3 ? (or 16 P —KB3 ?, R × P ch; 17 P × R, Q × P ch; 18 K—R1, R—Kt1 etc.), R × Kt; 17 Q—K2, R—

R5; 18 KR—K1, Q × RP ch; 19 K—B1, Q—R8 ch !; 20 B × Q, R × B mate!

16 . . . .   R × Q
17 KR × R !

The right Rook!

17 . . . .   P × Kt

"And now my good friend Fluess leaned back as who should say, 'The ending isn't easy, to be sure, but we'll find a way.' " (Nimzovich)

18 P—B5 !

Threatens mate in two!

18 . . . .   R—Kt1

Or 18 . . . K—Kt1; 19 QR —Kt1 ch and mate next move.

19 QR—Kt1 !

Black resigns, as he is helpless against the threat of 20 B
—R6 mate. Nimzovich: "Never
shall I forget the comical look
of horror on my opponent's
face as he realized his plight."

4. He Who Vacillates is Lost

THE TEXTBOOKS emphasize the importance of planning;
good advice, but not always easy to take. Sometimes a
position lacks character, making it difficult to formulate a
plan. Other times, a choice must be made between two or
more plans. In some cases, it is essential to defer making a
choice.

It was in these unclear positions that Nimzovich dis-
played an unrivalled mastery. He was inimitable in the art
of keeping all possibilities open, and it is just this strategy
which is the key to some of his most "mysterious" games.
How rare an art this is, may be seen from Schlechter's disastrous preoccupation with two distinct plans in the following game.

RUY LOPEZ

Carlsbad, 1907

WHITE: *C. Schlechter*   BLACK: *A. Nimzovich*

1 P—K4	P—K4
2 Kt—KB3	Kt—QB3
3 B—Kt5	P—QR3
4 B—R4	Kt—B3
5 Kt—B3	B—Kt5

Good enough, although the
moderns prefer 5 . . . P—

QKt4; 6 B—Kt3, B—K2.

6 Kt—Q5	B—K2
7 O—O	O—O

7 . . . Kt × P can lead to
trouble after the opening of
the King file by 8 P—Q4.

[13

8 R—K1   P—Q3
9 Kt × Kt *ch*

The Knight must make a decision sooner or later. 9 Kt × B *ch* gives White two Bishops, but at the cost of removing a piece which is not very useful to Black.

9 . . . .   B × Kt
10 P—B3   P—KR3

Apparently incomprehensible. Nimzovich does not want to embark on a definite course of action until Schlechter has committed himself.

11 P—KR3   Kt—K2
12 P—Q4   Kt—Kt3
13 B—K3   K—R2

Still waiting.

14 Q—Q2   B—K3
15 B—B2   Q—K2

White has three possible plans:

I. He can play P × P, opening the Queen file and permitting wholesale exchanges on that file. This drawish course does not appeal to Schlechter.

II. He can play P—Q5 followed by a general Queen-side advance: P—B4 followed by P—QKt4, intending the eventual P—B5. Black has fair defensive resources, and can react strongly by preparing for . . . P—KB4.

III. He can prepare for P—KB4 himself. The necessary preliminaries for this advance would have to be elaborate.

16 P—Q5

Schlechter appears to have decided in favor of the second plan.

16 . . . .   B—Q2
17 K—R2

. . . But he vacillates! Now Schlechter flirts with the idea of playing P—KB4 after all.

17 . . . .   Kt—R1 !

This queer-looking retreat is explained by the following

move. Schlechter must have been puzzled!

| 18 Kt—Kt1 | P—KKt4 |
| 19 P—KKt3 | Kt—Kt3 |

A hot fight is being waged around the possibility of advancing the King's Bishop Pawn. If now 20 P—KB4?, KtP × P; 21 P × P, P × P (not 21 . . . Kt × P?; 22 B × Kt, P × B; 23 P—K5 *ch* winning a piece); 22 B × P, Kt × B; 23 P—K5 *ch* (23 Q × Kt?? loses the Queen), Kt—Kt3 and Black comes out a Pawn ahead.

| 20 Q—Q1 | B—Kt2 |
| 21 Q—B3 | P—QR4 ! |

Very subtle: he prevents P—QKt4 as a follow-up to P—B4. Hence Schlechter renounces all further Queen-side ambitions and redoubles his efforts on the other wing.

| 22 Kt—K2 | B—Kt4 ! |

Another crafty move: if White's Queen retreats to make room for P—KB4, that advance can be met by . . . B × Kt, winning a Pawn.

| 23 P—QR4 | B—Q2 |

Now Queen-side action by White is blocked for good.

24 R—R1 !

Intending to open the King's Rook file by P—R4, at the cost of a Pawn.

24 . . . .   Q—K1 !

So that if 25 P—R4, Q—B1 ! threatening to win with . . . B—Kt5. Or if 25 P—KKt4, Kt—R5; 26 Q—Kt3, P—KB3 followed by . . . P—R4 with the initiative.

25 P—R4	Q—B1 !
26 B—Q3	B—Kt5
27 Q—Kt2	P × P
28 P—B3	P—R6 !
29 Q—B1	

Schlechter has played cleverly and appears to have attained his objective; for if now 29 . . . B—Q2; 30 P—KKt4 followed by 31 Q × P with a devastating attack.

29 . . . . · · · · · · · P—KB4 *!*
30 P × B

Despair. After 30 Kt—Kt1 a likely continuation is 30 . . . P—B5; 31 P × P, P × P; 32 B—Q2, B—Q2; 33 Kt × P, Q—Q1 *!*; 34 B—K1 (or 34 Q —B2, B—KB3 *!* with a winning position), Q—K1; 35 P —Kt3, Kt—K4; 36 B—K2, Q—R4 and White cannot hold out much longer.

30 . . . . · · · · · · · P × KP
31 Q × P · · · · · · · P × B
32 B × P

Surrendering to the inevitable: if 32 Kt—Kt1, P—K5 *!*; 33 K—Kt2 (33 B × P is answered as in the text), Kt— K4; 35 B × P, Q × P and wins.

32 . . . . · · · · · · · R—R1 *!*

Just as conclusive as . . . P × Kt. White resigns, as he loses a piece without compensation. One of Nimzovich's most profound games!

Final Position

5. "The Soul of Chess"

WHEN Philidor announced that the Pawns were the soul of chess, his contemporaries listened respectfully but were mystified. Almost a century passed before Steinitz clarified the statement of his great predecessor. Nimzovich had the historic task of popularizing this concept so widely that today even quite weak players are familiar with the importance of Pawn positions.

SCOTCH GAME

Hamburg, 1910

WHITE: *A. Nimzovich*   BLACK: *R. Spielmann*

1	P—K4	P—K4
2	Kt—KB3	Kt—QB3
3	P—Q4	P × P
4	Kt × P	Kt—B3

This opening has virtually disappeared from tournament play because it presents Black with too many equalizing opportunities.

5	Kt—QB3	B—Kt5
6	Kt × Kt	KtP × Kt
7	B—Q3	P—Q4
8	P × P	P × P

By interpolating 8 . . . Q —K2 *ch* Black virtually has a draw for the asking. But an attacking player like Spielmann naturally shuns such simplifying possibilities.

9	O—O	O—O
10	B—KKt5	P—B3
11	Kt—K2	

Nowadays 11 Q—B3 is the favored move.

[17

11 . . . .   R—K1

An excellent alternative is
11 . . . B—Q3 *!* (threatens 12
. . . B × P *ch*); 12 Kt—Kt3 *?*
(better 12 Kt—Q4), P—KR3 *!;*
13 B—Q2, Kt—Kt5 *!;* 14 B—
K2 (not 14 P—KR3 *?*, Kt × P;
15 K × Kt, Q—R5; 16 Q—B3,
P—KB4 followed by . . . P
—B5 regaining the piece advantageously), Q—R5; 15 B
× Kt, B × B (Steinitz—Zuker-
tort, Match, 1886) and Black
has decidedly the better game.

12 Kt—Q4   Q—Q3
13 Q—B3   Kt—K5
14 B—K3   B—Q2
15 QR—Q1   Q—Kt3

Threatening . . . B—Kt5.
Black has an aggressive development, but his Pawn position
is shaky. This is the crucial
point about which the coming
play revolves.

16 P—KR3   B—Q3
17 B—B1 *!*

Unimpressed by Black's excellent development, Nimzovich prepares to undermine
the Queen's Pawn.

17 . . . .   R—K2

18 P—B4 *!*

The critical position. Rather
than allow himself to be bur-
dened with an isolated Pawn,
Spielmann advances boldly.

18 . . . .   P—QB4
19 Kt—K2   P—Q5
20 B—B4

Despite the superficially favorable impression created by
Black's position, Nimzovich
demonstrates that the center
Pawns are *still* weak!

20 . . . .   B—B3
21 Kt—Kt3 *!*

Clears the air: 21 . . . Kt
× Kt *?* is refuted by 22 Q ×
B *!* and wins.

21 . . . .   B × B

22 Q × B   Kt × Kt

So that if 23 B × Q?, Kt—
K7 *ch* wins a piece.

23 P × Kt   Q—K3 ?

Plausible as this move seems,
it proves fatal. 23 . . . B—
K5! gave drawing chances.

24 Q—B5!   P—Kt3

Or 24 . . . Q × Q; 25 R
× Q and Black loses a Pawn
with no counterplay.

25 Q × P

So the Queen's Pawn is isolated after all!

25 . . . .   R—Q1
26 K—R2   Q—Q2
27 R—B4!   R—K3 ! ?

Realizing that after 27 . . .
R(2)—K1; 28 B × P!, RP ×
B; 29 R(4) × QP, Q—B1; 30
R × R, R × R; 31 R × R *ch*,
Q × R; 32 Q × B the ending is
child's play, Spielmann hopes
for a "swindle." But his opponent's powerful position is
fool-proof against surprises.

28 B × P!   R—K7 ! ?

Capturing the Bishop is
ruinous because of 29 R(4) ×
QP.

29 B × BP *ch*! K—Kt2

If 29 . . . Q × B; 30 Q—
Kt5 *ch*! wins; or if 29 . . . K
—R1; 30 R—B2!!, R × R (if
30 . . . R—K2; 31 R × P! or
30 . . . R—K6; 31 B—Q5!
or 30 . . . R—K5; 31 B—
Q5!); 31 Q—K5 *ch* and mate
follows!

30 Q—Kt5 *ch* K—B1
31 B—R5 *ch*! Resigns

Spielmann has been beaten
with his own weapons!

6. Clash of Temperaments

ONE could not imagine two men more unlike than Nimzovich and Marshall. Whereas Nimzovich always searched painstakingly for the hidden finesse which was the subtle solution to even the simplest problems, Marshall generally relied on an intuitive but often phenomenally accurate appraisal of even the most difficult positions. It is symptomatic of the profoundly mysterious character of chess that Marshall's method proved effective so often.

Remarkably enough, Marshall achieved an excellent lifetime score in his games with Nimzovich. One may reasonably conjecture that Marshall's easygoing ways irritated Nimzovich and thus prevented him from doing his best. Marshall was an elemental force of nature, Nimzovich was a seeker after eternal truths.

QUEEN'S PAWN OPENING

Hamburg, 1910

WHITE: *A. Nimzovich*

BLACK: *F. J. Marshall*

1 P—Q4	P—Q4
2 Kt—KB3	P—QB4
3 P—B4	BP × P

3 . . . P—K3 transposes into the Tarrasch Defense. The text, on the other hand, leads to one of those quasi-symmetrical positions in which the advantage of the first move can be made to tell by refined play.

| 4 P × P | Q—R4 *ch* |

Black has saddled himself with an unrewarding task: he must work hard in order to obtain no more than equality. However, if 4 . . . Q × P; 5 Kt—B3 followed by 6 Kt × P or 6 Q × P with a considerable lead in development.

| 5 Q—Q2 *!* | Q × Q *ch* |

The exchange turns out badly, but if 5 . . . Q × QP; 6 Kt—B3 etc.

6 B × Q	Kt—KB3
7 Kt × P	Kt × P
8 Kt—Kt5 !	

Exploiting his advantage in development. The simplicity of the position is deceptive.

8 . . . .   Kt—R3

He has no choice, for if 8 . . . P—QR3; 9 P—K4 !, B—Q2 (9 . . . P × Kt loses a Pawn); 10 P × Kt, P × Kt (if 10 . . . B × Kt; 11 B × B *ch*, P × B; 12 Kt—B3, P—Kt5; 13 Kt—Kt5 winning a Pawn); 11 Kt—B3, P—Kt5; 12 Kt—Kt5 with marked advantage.

9 QKt—B3   KKt—Kt5

If 9 . . . Kt × Kt; 10 B × Kt and the position is much in White's favor.

| 10 R—B1 | P—K3 |
| 11 P—QR3 | Kt—B3 |

Black's development is inferior. The position of his Queen's Knight is particularly unfortunate.

12 P—KKt3 !   B—Q2

Protecting himself as best he can against White's threat of posting his Bishop very strongly on the long diagonal. Most players would now continue 13 B—Kt2, but Nimzovich has a stronger line:

13 Kt—K4 !   Kt—K4 !

Cleverly guarding against the threatened Kt—Q6 *ch* (13 . . . O—O—O was out of the question).

| 14 Kt(4)—Q6 *ch* | B × Kt |
| 15 Kt × B *ch* | K—K2 |

If now 16 Kt × KtP ? ?, B—B3. But Nimzovich has a powerful refutation.

It requires a really imaginative player to search for complications in such a "simple" position.

[21

16 P—B4 *!!*   Kt—B3

Other moves are no better:
I 16 . . . K × Kt; 17 P × Kt
ch, K × P; 18 B—Kt2 *!* with a
winning game.
II 16 . . . B—B3; 17 P ×
Kt *!*, B × R; 18 P—K4, KR—
QKt1 (if 18 . . . B—B6; 19
K—B2, B—R4; 20 Kt × KtP,
Kt—Kt1; 21 R—B7 *ch* and
Black can resign); 19 P—
QKt4 *!*, P—B3 (else P—Kt5);
20 B × Kt, P × B; 21 R—B7
ch, K—Q1 (if 21 . . . K—
B1; 22 P × P and Black is lost,
for example 22 . . . R—Kt3;
23 R—B7 *ch*, K—Kt1; 24 R ×
P *ch*, K—B1; 25 B—R6 *!*, R ×
Kt; 26 R × QRP *ch* and mate
follows); 22 R × KtP winning
easily.
16 . . . Kt—Kt3 was prob-
ably best.

22]

17 Kt × KtP *!!* QR—QKt1

On 17 . . . KR—QKt1 Nim-
zovich intended 18 B—Kt2 *!*,
R × Kt; 19 R × Kt *!* and wins.

18 Kt—R5	Kt × Kt
19 B × Kt	R × P
20 B—B3	R—Kt6
21 B × P	R—QB1

Or 21 . . . R—KKt1; 22
B—Q4 retaining his material
advantage.

22 R × R	B × R
23 B—Q4	R × RP
24 B × P	B—Kt2
25 R—Kt1	K—Q3

Black remains a Pawn down
without compensation.

26 K—B2	B—Q4
27 B—R3	Kt—Kt5

28 B—Kt8 *ch*   K—Q2
29 R—Q1   K—B1 ?

Losing a piece; but if 29
. . . K—K1 (29 . . . K—B3;
30 R—B1 *ch*); 30 B—Q6 with
a fairly easy win.

30 B—Q6 !   R—R5
31 B × Kt   Resigns

For if 31 . . . R × B; 32
R × B.

7. Style

"THE STYLE is the man himself," says Buffon, and nowhere
is the famous phrase (*Le style est l'homme même*) more
appropriate than in chess. Many men, many styles; and
what is chess style but the intangible expression of the will
to win? The universe of the chessmaster is not without its
grimmer aspects, for it is a world of dog-eat-dog. Beauty in
chess (like virtue) is its own reward; it is only the incidental
by-product of relentless struggle.

In such an atmosphere, the quality of objective appreciation is not seen too frequently. Yet differences in style
may produce queer paradoxes. Thus Vidmar, always a
thoroughly orthodox player and often a colorless one, was
among the first to recognize and admire Nimzovich's blazing
originality.

In this respect Vidmar showed to advantage, for it is a
wise man who knows his own style. Dullards fancy them-

[23

selves as combinative geniuses; others who enmesh themselves in mazes of complexity, preen themselves on their straightforward play.

PHILIDOR'S DEFENSE

San Sebastian, 1911

WHITE: *R. Teichmann*   BLACK: *A. Nimzovich*

1 P—K4	P—K4
2 Kt—KB3	P—Q3
3 P—Q4	Kt—KB3

An interpolation, popularized by Nimzovich, which gave this venerable defense a temporary lease on life. Today it is well known that after 4 P × P, Kt × P; 5 Q—Q5, Kt—B4; 6 B—Kt5 White remains with a marked initiative.

4 Kt—B3	QKt—Q2
5 B—QB4	B—K2
6 O—O	O—O

The alternative method of not castling also has its drawbacks (see Game 19).

7 Q—K2	P—B3

This "Hanham" formation is not to everyone's taste, as it leads to a sadly cramped position. But it is a line which is full of finesse.

8 B—KKt5

A thoughtless "developing" move which allows Black a free hand on the Queen-side. Necessary was 8 P—QR4*!* preventing Black's expansion by . . . P—QKt4 and leaving White with a fine game.

8	P—KR3
9 B—R4	Kt—R4 *!*

Giving White a cruel choice: parting with the two Bishops or freeing Black's game with

10 B × B, Q × B; 11 P—KKt3,
Kt—Kt3; 12 B—Kt3, B—Kt5
etc.

10	B—KKt3	Kt × B
11	RP × Kt	P—QKt4
12	B—Q3	P—R3

Neutralizing the disorganiz-
ing effect of P—Q5 and/or P
—R4. We can now see that
White's omission of 8 P—QR4
was a serious lapse.

13	P—R4	B—Kt2
14	QR—Q1	Q—B2 !

Nimzovich is too old a hand
to be taken in by the possibility 14 . . . KP × P; 15 Kt ×
QP, P—QB4 (winning a piece
—so it seems!); 16 Kt—B5, P
—B5; 17 Q—Kt4 ! and White's
game is positionally won.

15	RP × P	RP × P
16	P—KKt4	

Teichmann expects to play
P—KKt3, K—Kt2, R—KR1
and eventually P—Kt5. The
way in which Nimzovich
snatches the King Rook file
for himself and operates on
the other wing at the same
time is really fascinating.

16	. . . .	KR—K1

The presence of this dis-
agreeable adversary for White's
Queen provokes the following
reply.

17	P—Q5	P—Kt5
18	P × P	B × P
19	Kt—Kt1	Kt—B4
20	QKt—Q2	Q—B1 !

The process by which Nim-
zovich steadily increases the
pressure makes the coming
play highly instructive. White
crumbles imperceptibly.

21	B—B4	P—Kt3

Naturally avoiding the simple trap 21 . . . Q × P; 22 B
× P ch and at the same time
furthering his long-range plans.

22	P—KKt3	K—Kt2
23	Kt—R2	B—KKt4 !

[25

This Bishop cannot be driven away from his commanding position; for if 24 P—B4, P × P; 25 P × P, B—B3 and a Pawn falls.

24 P—KB3	Q—B2
25 KR—K1	R—R1 !
26 Kt(Q2)—B1	P—R4 !
27 P × P	R × P

Now Black has the open King Rook file at his disposal. Passive defense and simplification are the order of the day for his opponent.

28 B—Q5	QR—R1
29 B × B	Q × B
30 Q—B4	Q—Kt3 !
31 K—Kt2	Kt—K3

Apparently Black is only interested in getting his Knight

to Q5. Actually he is plotting a diabolical combination: 32 . . . R × Kt *ch* ! !; 33 Kt × R, R × Kt *ch;* 34 K × R, Q—B7 *ch;* 35 K—R3, B—B5 !; 36 KR—Kt1, Kt—Kt4 *ch* and mate follows!

| 32 R—K2 | Kt—Q5 |

Forcing the Rook off the second rank, for if 33 R—B2, B—K6 ! is crushing.

| 33 R(2)—K1 | Q—Kt2 ! |

If now 34 P—B3 (the threat was 34 . . . R—QB1), P × P; 35 P × P (or 35 Q × P, R—QB1 etc.), Q—Kt7 *ch* etc. and White must resign.

| 34 R × Kt | P × R |
| 35 Kt—Kt4 | |

35 Q × QP *ch*, B—B3; 36 Q × QP, R—Q1 is likewise without long-term prospects for White.

35	Q—Kt3
36 P—B4	B—K2
37 R—Q1	P—B4 !

Now it is Black who wants exchanges. The text clears the atmosphere.

38 Kt—B2	P × P
39 Q × P *ch*	Q × Q
40 R × Q	P—Q4
41 P—Kt4	B—B4 *!*

More simplification.

42 R—Q1	R—R5
43 R × P	B × Kt

44 K × B	R × P
45 K—K3	R—QB1 *!*

So that if 46 R—Q4, R ×
QBP; 47 R × KtP, R—Kt8 and
wins.

46 K × P	R—B5 *ch*
47 K—Q3	R(B5) × KBP

The rest is easy:

48 Kt—K3	R—Kt6
49 R—K5	K—B3
50 R—K8	K—B2
51 R—K5	R—B3
52 P—B4	P—Kt6
53 K—K4	R—K3
54 R × R	K × R
55 Kt—Q5	P—Kt4
Resigns	

8. "Lightning"

IN LIGHTNING or rapid-transit chess the modern expert has his opportunity to vie with the old masters. It is a pity that the brilliancies which are produced in these brief moments rarely see the light of day. An idea of what present-day masters can produce in ten-second chess is seen in the following game, which was played in a few leisure moments during a great tournament. The whole game must have taken some five minutes!

FOUR KNIGHTS' GAME

Carlsbad, 1911

WHITE: *A. Nimzovich*   BLACK: *Dr. S. Tartakover*

1	P—K4	P—K4
2	Kt—KB3	Kt—QB3
3	Kt—B3	Kt—B3
4	B—Kt5	B—Kt5
5	O—O	Kt—Q5

Black confuses two distinct variations. The text looks attractive, as it threatens to win a piece. Yet, if Black wanted to move the Knight, he should have played 4 . . . Kt—Q5.

6 Kt × Kt *!*   P × Kt
7 P—K5

This Pawn sacrifice yields a powerful attack.

7 . . . .   P × Kt
8 QP × P   B—K2

If 8 . . . B × P?; 9 P × B, Kt—Kt1; 10 B—R3 with a won game.

9 P × Kt   B × P

Likewise after 9 . . . P ×
P; 10 R—K1 Black's position
is very difficult.

10 R—K1 *ch*   K—B1

Or 10 . . . B—K2; 11 Q—
K2, P—QB3; 12 B—Q3, P—
Q4; 13 B—KKt5, P—B3; 14
Q—R5 *ch* with a powerful at-
tack.

11 B—QB4   P—Q3

11 . . . P—B3 had to be
tried here, in order to break
the Bishop's diagonal with
. . . P—Q4.

12 Q—R5   P—KKt3
13 B—R6 *ch*   B—Kt2

This leads to immediate dis-
aster, but if 13 . . . K—Kt1;
14 B × P *ch* forces mate ·in
two: 14 . . . K × B; 15 Q—
Q5 *ch*, B—K3; 16 Q × B mate.
But Black's days are numbered
in any event.

14 Q—B3

Astonishing as it may seem
at such an early stage, Black is
already defenseless! The extra
Pawn is meaningless.

14 . . . .   Q—Q2

If 14 . . . P—KB3; 15 R—
K8 *ch* ! !, K × R (if 15 . . . Q
× R; 16 Q × P *ch* and mate
next move); 16 B × B with a
winning position.

15 Q—KB6 !   KR—Kt1

Forced!

16 B × B *ch*   R × B

Now it seems that he is mo-
mentarily out of danger.

17 B × P ! !   Resigns

If 17 . . . R × B; 18 Q—
R8 mate, or 17 . . . Q × B;
18 Q—Q8 *ch* and mate next
move. A good example of the
dangers of Pawn-grabbing in
the opening, especially ·in
speed chess.

9. Deceptive Appearances

PERHAPS Chajes would not have pounced on the win of the exchange so readily if he had been familiar with the famous couplet from *H. M. S. Pinafore*:

> Things are seldom what they seem.
> Skim milk masquerades as cream.

True, in this game, Nimzovich turns the lines inside out; for what seems to be a naive blunder, turns out to be the beginning of a far-sighted combination.

SICILIAN DEFENSE

Carlsbad, 1911

WHITE: *A. Nimzovich*   BLACK: *O. Chajes*

| 1 P—K4 | P—QB4 |
| 2 P—QB3 | Kt—QB3 |

For 2 . . . P—K3 see Game 12.

3 P—Q4	P × P
4 P × P	P—Q4
5 P × P	Q × P

Black's game looks promising, but in order to maintain his Queen at its present commanding post, he will have to allow his opponent the two Bishops.

| 6 Kt—KB3 | P—K4 |

7 Kt—B3	B—QKt5
8 B—Q2	B × Kt
9 B × B	P—K5

Probably best, as it curbs the power of White's Queen Bishop. The alternative 9 . . . P × P; 10 Kt × P, Kt—B3 (10 . . . Kt × Kt; 11 Q × Kt gives White an ideal two-Bishop position); 11 Kt × Kt, Q × Kt (else he is left with a weak Pawn on the open Queen's Bishop file); 12 B—Kt4! is not good for Black.

| 10 Kt—K5 | Kt × Kt |

White was threatening 11
B—B4.

11 P × Kt　　　　　Kt—K2

11 . . . Q × Q *ch;* 12 R ×
Q gives White too powerful a
position.

12 Q—R4 *ch*　　B—Q2
13 Q—R3

Nimzovich's Queen maneu-
ver, intended to create difficulties in Black's castling, succeeds because Chajes counters
weakly.

13 . . . .　　　　P—K6 *?*

The right way, says Schlechter, is 13 . . . Q—K3 and if
14 R—Q1, O—O; 15 R—Q6,
Q—B4.

14 P—B3 *!*　　　Q—K3

15 R—Q1 *!*　　　Kt—B4

Nimzovich has cleverly exploited his opponent's inexactitude: if 15 . . . O—O *?;* 16
R—Q6, Q—B4; 17 B—Q3. So
Chajes decides to embark on
dubious adventures.

16 B—Q3　　　Q—KKt3 *! ?*

Setting two subtle traps.

The first trap: if 17 P—
KKt4 *?*, Q—R3; 18 B × Kt,
Q—R5 *ch;* 19 K—K2, Q—B7
ch; 20 K—Q3, B—Kt4 *ch;* 21
K—K4, B—B3 *ch* with at
least a draw.

17 O—O *!*

"Falling" into the second
trap.

17 . . . .　　　　P—K7

18 B × P   Kt—K6

Wins the exchange—at a price.

19 K—B2 *!*   Kt × R *ch*

Forced, for if 19 . . . Kt × R; 20 P—K6 *!*, P × P (if 20 . . . Q × P; 21 B × Kt with the decisive threat 22 R—K1; or if 20 . . . B × P; 21 B—Kt5 *ch* and wins); 21 R × B *!*, K × R; 22 B—Kt5 *ch*, K—B2; 23 Q—B5 *ch*, K—Q1; 24 Q—Q6 *ch* and mate in two.

20 R × Kt   Q—Kt3 *ch*

To forestall P—K6; but his King is left stranded in the center.

21 B—Q4   Q—K3
22 P—QKt3 *!*   B—B3
23 B—B5   Q—B4

After 23 . . . Q × KP the opening of the King file is fatal.

24 Q—B1 *!*   R—Q1
25 B—Q6   P—KR4

Or 25 . . . R × B; 26 P × R, O—O; 27 Q—K3 with a winning game.

26 B—Q3   Q—K3
27 Q—Kt5 *!*

27 . . . .   R—Q2

Capitulation; but if 27 . . . P—KKt3; 28 B—B4, Q—Q2; 29 P—K6 *!*, P × P; 30 B—R3 *!*, Q—QB2; 31 Q × P *ch* and Black can resign.

28 B—KB5   R × B

Or 28 . . . Q—R3; 29 B × R *ch* with a quick mate.

29 P × R   P—B3

If 29 . . . Q—B3; 30 Q—K3 *ch* is deadly.

30 Q—Kt6 *ch*   Q—B2
31 P—Q7 *ch*   B × P
32 Q × Q *ch*   Resigns

A game out of the ordinary.

10. Originality as a Chore

FAMOUS as he was for originality, Nimzovich really out-did himself in this game. Even so staunchly orthodox a critic as Leopold Hoffer, editor of the famous column in "The Field," was enchanted with Nimzovich's play.

And more remarkable than Nimzovich's originality, per-haps, is his conscientious attitude: he deliberately sets him-self an inordinately difficult technical task, and carries it through flawlessly. At the end he triumphs with one of his typically piquant creations. Once more his favorite Knights carry off the honors.

FRENCH DEFENSE

Carlsbad, 1911

WHITE: *A. Nimzovich*		BLACK: *G. Levenfish*
1 P—K4	P—K3	
2 P—Q4	P—Q4	
3 P—K5	P—QB4	
4 P—QB3	Kt—QB3	
5 Kt—B3	P—B3	

Wrong, says Nimzovich. He should continue the attack on the *base* of the Pawn-chain with 5 . . . Q—Kt3 as in Game 11.

6 B—QKt5

Anticipating a later block-ade on K5, he plans to remove Black's protective Knight.

6 . . . .   B—Q2

Threatening to win a Pawn.

7 O—O !

7 . . . .   Q—Kt3

Very discreet. On 7 . . .
Kt × KP Nimzovich intended
8 Kt × Kt, B × B; 9 Q—R5
ch, K—K2; 10 Q—B7 *ch*, K—
Q3; 11 P × P *ch!*, K × Kt; 12
R—K1 *ch*, K—B4; 13 Q—R5
ch, P—Kt4; 14 P—Kt4 mate!

8 B × Kt   P × B
9 KP × P   Kt × P

A superficially attractive developing move. He might have
been better off to guard his
K4 with 9 . . . KtP × P.

10 Kt—K5 !   B—Q3
11 P × P   B × P
12 B—Kt5 !

Preventing Black from playing . . . O—O. The blockade
on K5, which is also slated to
appear in Game 11, is now
fully established.

12 . . . .   Q—Q1
13 B × Kt !

Heresy! White is left with
two Knights against two Bishops.

13 . . . .   Q × B
14 Q—R5 *ch!*

Forcing a weakening of the
black squares which will be
useful later on.

14 . . . .   P—Kt3
15 Q—K2   R—Q1

Or 15 . . . B—Q3; 16 P—
KB4, B × Kt; 17 P × B and
White's control of the King
Bishop file and the black
squares will prove decisive.

16 Kt—Q2   O—O
17 QR—K1   KR—K1
18 K—R1

In order to intensify his grip
on K5 by playing P—KB4.

18 . . . .   B—Q3
19 P—KB4   P—B4

20 P—B4

Nimzovich later decided that 20 Q—R6 would have been even stronger. However, the text poses a serious problem for Black, as 20 . . . P —Q5 would give K4 to White's pieces and imprison the King's Bishop.

20 . . . .   B—KB1 *? !*
21 P × P   B—B1

But not 21 . . . P × P *? ?*; 22 Kt × B and wins.

22 Kt—K4   Q—Kt2
23 P × P *? !*

With 23 P—Q6 *!* Nimzovich would have obtained a decisive positional advantage. The text, on the other hand, permits the Bishops to become dangerously mobile.

23 . . . .   B × P
24 Q—R6   K—R1
25 R—Q1   B—Kt1

Best, for if 25 . . . B—Q4; 26 Kt—QB3, B—R1 (not 26 . . . Q—Kt2 *?*; 27 Q × Q, B × Q; 28 R × R, R × R; 29 Kt —B7 *ch*); 27 Kt—Kt5 with strong pressure.

26 P—QKt3   R—Q5 *!*

27 R × R *!*   P × R
28 Q—R5   R—B1

Now that . . . R—Q1 has been prevented, Black takes the open file. The position seems ideal for the Bishops.

29 R—Q1   R—B7
30 P—KR3   Q—Kt2
31 R × P   B—B4

White is apparently lost, for if 32 R—R4, B—Kt3; 33 Q— K1, B—Q4. But Nimzovich has calculated everything to a hair, relying on the powerful centralized position of his Knights.

32 Q—Q8 *! !*   B—K2

And not 32 . . . B × R; 33 Q × B, Q—Kt2; 34 Kt—Q6 *! !* and there is no defense against

[35

the threatened 35 Kt—K8!
The text is a necessary parry
to the menace of 33 R—Q7.

33 Q—Q7   Q—R3
34 R—Q3 !

Guards against Black's mating threat, and provides for
Q—Q4.

34 . . . .   B—B1
35 Kt—B7 *ch*   B × Kt

If 35 . . . K—Kt2; 36 Q—
Q4 *ch !* and mate in two!

36 Q × B   R—B1
37 R—Q7   Resigns

A beautiful finish.

11.   *World Premiere*

OF THIS game Nimzovich later wrote in *My System*, "A
most instructive game from A to Z, one which I regard
as the first in which my new philosophy of the center was
exhibited."

It should be borne in mind that Nimzovich's play here
was so revolutionary that it earned him little more than contempt. Few critics were able to appreciate the fine points
of the game.

FRENCH DEFENSE

Carlsbad, 1911

WHITE: *A. Nimzovich*   BLACK: *G. Salve*

1 P—K4   P—K3
2 P—Q4   P—Q4
3 P—K5 ! ?

An old continuation favored

by Steinitz. In 1911 the move
had been absent from tournament play for almost a quarter
of a century, as a result of
Tarrasch's "refutation" in 1888.

3 . . . .   P—QB4

Can White maintain his
grip on K5 and work up a
King-side attack as a result?—
or can Black smash the Pawn-
chain by means of the text and
eventually . . . P—B3 . . . ?

4 P—QB3

Later on Nimzovich dis-
carded this move in favor of
4 Kt—KB3 or 4 Q—Kt4.

4 . . . .   Kt—QB3
5 Kt—B3   Q—Kt3
6 B—Q3

6 B—K2 is more accurate,
as will become apparent later.

6 . . . .   B—Q2 ?

Salve of course realizes that
he cannot win a Pawn by 6
. . . P × P; 7 P × P, Kt ×
QP?; 8 Kt × Kt, Q × Kt??
because of 9 B—Kt5 ch winning the Queen. The proper
course, however, is 6 . . . P
× P; 7 P × P, B—Q2 as in
Game 12, to which the reader
is referred for a full exposition
of that variation.

In playing the text, Salve is
gratified at the cruel alternative which faces White: either
loss of tempo with 7 B—K2,
or giving up the center with 7
P × P and allowing Black to
develop with gain of time (7
. . . B × P).

What is Nimzovich's choice
to be? *This is one of the most
dramatic moments in the history of chess!*

7 P × P *!!*

For this move, one of the
deepest ever played, Nim-
zovich was roundly damned
by the chess world.

7 . . . .   B × P
8 O—O

If Salve could have fore-
seen what was coming, he
would now have played 8 . . .

P—QR4 to maintain his King Bishop's position.

8 . . . .   P—B3

Logical, consistent and . . . all wrong!

9 P—QKt4 ! !

This ugly move is based on a profound understanding of the position. Black wants to remove the hostile King's Pawn, after which he can develop freely. Nimzovich wants to demonstrate that the disappearance of his center Pawns will be compensated for by the occupation of Q4 and K5 by *pieces*. These pieces will *blockade* the later advance of Black's Queen Pawn and King Pawn, so that his game will remain constricted. But how can these ideas (which were completely unknown in 1911!) be carried out?

The obvious move is 9 Q—K2, but after 9 . . . P × P; 10 Kt × P, Kt × Kt; 11 Q × Kt, Kt—B3 Black's development is satisfactory; he will eventually drive away the Queen and play . . . P—K4; and the White Queen Bishop cannot move because the Pawn at QKt2 must be guarded.

Nimzovich's last move is the brilliant solution: the Black Bishop is driven back, the QKtP no longer needs protection, the Queen Bishop is ready to take up his blockading duties.

9 . . . .   B—K2

Salve must have been delighted with this position: look at White's backward Queen Bishop Pawn on the open file!

10 B—KB4   P × P
11 Kt × P   Kt × Kt
12 B × Kt

The blockade of the King Pawn has now been established!

12 . . . .   **Kt—B3**

Many a tactical finesse is needed to maintain the blockade; thus 12 . . . B—KB3 is refuted by 13 Q—R5 *ch*, P—Kt3; 14 B × P *ch*, P × B; 15 Q × P *ch*, K—K2; 16 B × B *ch*, Kt × B; 17 Q—Kt7 *ch* and wins.

13 Kt—Q2 !

Nimzovich does not agree with Oscar Wilde's "I can resist everything but temptation." 13 Q—B2 looks attractive, for if 13 . . . O—O; 14 B × Kt, R × B; 15 B × P *ch*, K—R1; 16 B—Q3 and White has won a Pawn. *But he has given up the blockade,* and after 16 . . . P—K4 Black's strong center and pressure on

the weak QBP would go far in neutralizing the Pawn minus.

13 . . . .   **O—O**

Note how magnificently the centralized Bishop is functioning: it not only blockades the King Pawn—it also guards the Queen Bishop Pawn.

14 Kt—B3   **B—Q3**

But not 14 . . . B—Kt4 (trying to exchange the inferior Bishop); 15 B—Q4, Q —R3; 16 B × B, Q × B; 17 Kt—Kt5, Q—B3; 18 R—K1 winning the King Pawn. Such is the power of the blockade!

15 Q—K2 !

Always the most accurate! If 15 B—Q4, Q—B2; 16 Q—K2, Kt—Kt5 *!;* 17 P—KR3, P —K4 *!* and Black frees himself.

15 . . . .   **QR—B1**

Baffled but still optimistic, Salve seeks counterplay. The alternative 15 . . . QR—K1 and 16 . . . B—B1 is not attractive.

16 B—Q4   **Q—B2**

[39

17 Kt—K5   B—K1
18 QR—K1

Over-protecting the strong point K5. The blockade is crushing.

18 . . . .   B × Kt

Removing the paralyzing Knight, but exposing himself to the grip of the united Bishops. There is little choice: if 18 . . . Kt—Q2; 19 Kt × Kt, B × Kt; 20 Q—R5 wins.

19 B × B   Q—B3
20 B—Q4 !

Compelling Black's Bishop to choose one of the diagonals.

20 . . . .   B—Q2
21 Q—B2 !

Threatening to win a Pawn and thus gaining time for the further deployment of the Queen Rook.

21 . . . .   R—KB2

So as to answer 22 B × Kt with . . . P × B. Advancing one of the King-side Pawns would create a fatal weakness.

22 R—K3   P—QKt3

23 R—Kt3   K—R1

White was again threatening to win a Pawn. But even the text does not help.

24 B × RP !   P—K4 !

Apparently winning a piece, but Nimzovich slips out. If instead 24 . . . Kt × B; 25 Q—Kt6 ! (not 25 R—R3, R—B4; 26 P—Kt4, P—K4 ! !), K—Kt1; 26 B × KKtP, Kt—B1; 27 Q—R6, Kt—R2; 28 B—B6 *ch* and wins.

25 B—Kt6 !   R—K2
26 R—K1   Q—Q3
27 B—K3

But not 27 R(3)—K3 ?, Kt—Kt5!

27 . . . .   P—Q5

White seems to have involved himself in one of those dangerous reactions which often follow a gain of material. But Nimzovich avoids all difficulties by simplifying adroitly.

28 B—Kt5   R × P

Else 29 Q—Q1 ! follows.

29 R × R   P × R

30 Q × P	K—Kt1
31 P—QR3	K—B1
32 B—R4 !	B—K1
33 B—B5	Q—Q5

White's threat of 34 B—Kt3 was too strong.

34 Q × Q	P × Q
35 R × R	K × R
36 B—Q3	

Still blockading!

36	K—Q3
37 B × Kt	P × B
38 K—B1	B—B3
39 P—KR4 !	Resigns

With Black tied down by the passed King Rook Pawn, the ending is hopeless for him. A game that made chess history!

12. *Right and Wrong*

ONE of the most delicious forms of irony appears in human affairs when a man gets the right results for the wrong reasons. The following game, like the previous one, is one of the most dramatic played in the history of chess; for in this game Nimzovich, who never lacked courage, boldly adopted a much disputed variation against the great authority who was the leader of the anti-Nimzovich forces.

Yes, it required courage; for Tarrasch was a famous master, with the prestige of a notable career of more than two decades' duration. Yet Nimzovich did not shrink from the critical encounter, despite the hounding and ridicule which his startling theories had already brought upon his head.

The irony of the encounter lies in this: in the present instance, *the critics were right and Nimzovich was wrong!* Yet his burning faith and courage carried him safely through the ordeal. The result was that even his enemies sang his praises after the game—although they had previously reviled him for his justly earned successes!

FRENCH DEFENSE

(in effect)

San Sebastian, 1912

WHITE: *A. Nimzovich*   BLACK: *Dr. S. Tarrasch*

1 P—K4   P—QB4

Psychologically very interesting. Here one would expect 1 . . . P—K3, in order to give Nimzovich the opportunity to play his favorite variation.

2 P—QB3

As pointed out in the notes to Game 9, this advance is weaker than the usual 2 Kt—KB3; but it had the merit (in Nimzovich's eyes) of making possible a transposition into the French Defense.

2 . . . .   P—K3

Apparently Tarrasch has had a change of heart: 2 . . . P—Q4 is perfectly correct, but if he plays it, he is branded by the whole chess world as having evaded the crucial test of his controversy with Nimzovich.

3 P—Q4   P—Q4
4 P—K5

Thus we arrive at the thorny variation after all! However, the transposition makes us feel that while Nimzovich is eager for a fight, Tarrasch is entering the struggle in a hesitant and reluctant mood.

4 . . . .   Kt—QB3
5 Kt—B3   Q—Kt3
6 B—Q3

Following Game 11. In later years, however, Nimzovich resorted to the more accurate 6

B—K2. Despite this improvement, the variation ultimately proved unworkable, necessitating a new line of play.

6 . . . .   P × P !
7 P × P   B—Q2
8 B—K2

After Black's last move, the base of White's Pawn-chain (his Queen's Pawn) requires additional protection.

8 . . . .   KKt—K2
9 P—QKt3   Kt—B4
10 B—Kt2   B—Kt5 ch
11 K—B1

Interposition would lose the Queen Pawn. White has to make substantial concessions to keep this Pawn alive.

11 . . . .   B—K2

Too tame. Nimzovich himself later suggested the following aggressive procedure: 11 . . . O—O *!;* 12 P—Kt4, Kt—R3; 13 R—Kt1, P—B3 *!;* 14 P × P, R × P *!;* 15 P—Kt5, R × Kt; 16 B × R, Kt—B4; 17 R—Kt4, and now there are two leading possibilities: 17 . . . B—K1 *!;* 18 Q—K2, QKt × P; 19 R × Kt, Kt × R; 20 Q—K5, B—Kt4 *ch;* 21 K—Kt2, Kt—B4; 22 B × P, P × B; 23 Q × Kt, R—KB1; 24 Q × QP *ch,* R—B2 *!;* 25 Q—Q4, B—B4 and wins (Nimzovich) or 17 . . . R—KB1; 18 P—QR4, K—R1 *!;* 19 Kt—R3, P—K4; 20 Kt—B2, KKt × P with a winning game (Edward Lasker).

If White avoids the vigorous 12 P—Kt4, Black plays . . . P—B3 just the same, obtaining a strong attacking formation with his well-placed pieces. The less energetic text gives White a breathing spell.

12 P—Kt3   P—QR4 *?*

Playing by rote: Tarrasch is following one of his famous games. . . . O—O and . . . P—B3 was still the preferable course.

13 P—QR4   QR—B1
14 B—Kt5   Kt—Kt5 *?*

Weak: 14 . . . Kt—R2; 15 B × B *ch* (or 15 B—Q3, O—O; 16 B × Kt, P × B followed by . . . P—B3), K × B gives Black a good game.

15 Kt—B3 *!*

Nimzovich's improvement on the famous game Paulsen—Tarrasch, Nuremberg, 1888, which ran 15 B × B *ch?*, K × B; 16 Kt—B3, Kt—B3; 17 Kt—QKt5, Kt—R2; 18 Kt × Kt *?* (18 Q—Q3 *!*), Q × Kt with a distinct positional plus for Black.

15 . . . .   Kt—QR3 *?*

Only now does Tarrasch realize that he has been outgeneraled by his sly opponent: the apparently decisive 15 . . . B × B ch; 16 Kt × B, Kt —B7 is refuted by 17 R—B1, Kt—K6 ch; 18 P × Kt, Kt × KP ch; 19 K—K2, Kt × Q; 20 R × R ch, K—Q2; 21 R × R, Kt × B; 22 R—QB1 !, B—Q1 (what else?); 23 R—B2.

But 15 . . . B × B ch; 16 Kt × B, O—O would still have left Black with a fine game.

16 K—Kt2   Kt—B2 ?

Again . . . B × B should be played.

17 B—K2 !

Rightly perceiving that his King Bishop will be more useful than Black's Queen Bishop.

17	**B—Kt5**
18 Kt—R2	**Kt—QR3**
19 B—Q3	**Kt—K2 ?**

Tarrasch must be demoralized. It cannot be good policy to allow the exchange of the precious King Bishop. Later this piece will be missed.

20 QR—B1	**Kt—B3**
21 Kt × B	**Kt(R3) × Kt**
22 B—Kt1 !	

Nimzovich, of course, does not imitate his opponent's mistake: he conserves the King Bishop because of the resulting King-side attacking chances.

22 . . . .   P—R3

Tarrasch is rightly afraid to castle, which would give White a winning attack: 22 . . . O—O ?; 23 Kt—Kt5 and he forces a breach in Black's rampart of Pawns in front of the King.

23 P—Kt4 !   Kt—K2

Dr. Lasker, who was an expert at defending such uncomfortable positions, recommends the cold-blooded 23 . . . K—K2, with a more elastic defensive formation.

[45

24 R × R *ch*	B × R
25 Kt—K1	R—B1
26 Kt—Q3	P—B3

Seeking counterchances—rather late in the day.

27 Kt × Kt	Q × Kt
28 P × P	R × P
29 B—B1 *!*	

Now both Bishops are trained on the King-side.

29	Kt—B3 *P*

Edward Lasker recommends 29 . . . P—K4 *!;* 30 P—Kt5 (not 30 P × P *P*, B × P *!*), RP × P; 31 B × P, R—B2 with a draw as the likely result.

30 P—Kt5 !

Beginning the final attack.

30	P × P
31 B × P	R—B1
32 B—K3	Q—K2

If 32 . . . P—K4; 33 Q—R5 *ch* is disastrous for Black.

33 Q—Kt4 *!*	Q—B3
34 R—Kt1 *!*	R—R1
35 K—R1 *!*	

With his last three moves,

Nimzovich has strengthened his position decisively.

35	R—R5

Despair. Kmoch has claimed that 35 . . . K—B1 saves the game, but this is incorrect. There follows 36 R—Kt3 *!*, R —R5; 37 Q—Q1 *!!* (threatening 38 R—B3 or 38 B—Kt5), K—Kt1; 38 B—Kt5, Q × QP; 39 R—Q3, Q—K5 *ch;* 40 P— B3 and wins; or 36 . . . K— Kt1; 37 B—Kt5 *!*, Q—B2 (if 37 . . . Q × BP; 38 B—R6 *!* wins, or if 37 . . . Q × QP; 38 Q × Q, Kt × Q; 39 B—B6, Kt—B4; 40 B × Kt, P × B; 41 R × P *ch*, K—B1; 42 R—B7 etc.); 38 R—KB3, Q—K1 (if 38 . . . Q—R4; 39 Q—B4, Q—K1; 40 B—Kt6 *!*); 39 B— B6 and wins.

36 Q—Kt3 *!*   R × P

If he retreats the Rook to guard against the threat of 37 B—Kt5, then 37 Q × P wins easily.

37 B × R   Kt × B
38 Q × P   Q—B6 *ch*
39 Q—Kt2   Q × Q *ch*

White can always force the exchange of Queens with Q—Kt8 *ch.*

40 R × Q   Kt × P

If instead 40 . . . Kt—B4; 41 B × Kt, P × B; 42 P—R4, P—B5; 43 R—Kt8 *ch*, K—Q2; 44 R × B wins. Or 40 . . . Kt—B6; 41 R—Kt3, Kt—Q7; 42 P—R4, Kt × B; 43 P—R5 and the passed Pawn marches on.

41 P—R4   Resigns

A very absorbing game. The fact that 29 . . . P—K4 *!* would have saved Black is irritating, but it is part of what Dr. Bernstein has wittily called "the equalizing injustice of chess." 29 . . . P—K4 *!* was the logical sequel to the liberating move . . . P—B3.

13. Bishops on Opposite Colors

IN THE elementary books, we are taught that the presence of Bishops on opposite-colored squares "always" or generally leads to a draw. Nimzovich was one of the pioneers who demonstrated that many endings are won precisely because the Bishops are *not* on the same-colored squares.

What helped Nimzovich in his researches was his profound understanding of weak color complexes. Thus, the fact that his opponent's Bishop cannot guard the black squares in the following endgame is the key to White's subtle winning maneuvers.

FRENCH DEFENSE

Russian Championship—Vilna, 1912

WHITE: *A. Nimzovich* BLACK: *Dr. O. S. Bernstein*

1 P—K4	P—K3
2 P—Q4	P—Q4
3 P—K5	P—QB4
4 Kt—KB3	P × P
5 Q × P	Kt—QB3
6 Q—KB4	Q—B2
7 Kt—B3	

Two years later, in Game 16, Nimzovich experimented with 7 B—Kt5—which may be stronger than the text. As played, Black equalizes easily.

7	P—QR3

Preparing for . . . KKt—K2 by preventing Kt—QKt5.

8 B—Q3	KKt—K2
9 O—O	Kt—Kt3

Now White must part with his King's Bishop.

10 B × Kt	RP × B
11 Kt—K2 ?	

As Black has good counterplay (two Bishops, the open Rook file), White must play accurately. The text violates

48]

Nimzovich's rule of over-pro-
tection and allows the winning
reply 11 . . . Kt × P ! (and if
then 12 Q × Kt?? , B—Q3 !
wins the Queen, or if 12 Kt ×
Kt, B—Q3 regains the piece).

11 R—K1 should have been
played.

11	B—K2 ?
12 QKt—Q4	Kt × Kt
13 Q × Kt	

Surrendering a Pawn, for on
13 Kt × Kt, R—R5 is too
strong.

13	Q × BP
14 B—K3	Q—B5
15 Q × Q	P × Q
16 B—Kt6 !	

Despite his Pawn minus,
White has strong practical
chances. Black has an easy
draw, but winning is something else again.

| 16 . . . . | B—Q2 |

After 16 . . . B—Q1; 17
B × B, K × B Black's position
is very difficult.

| 17 KR—B1 | QR—B1 |
| 18 Kt—Q2 ! | B—KKt4 |

Apparently decisive, for if
19 Kt × P?, B × R; 20 Kt—
Q6 ch, K—K2; 21 Kt × R ch,
R × Kt and Black has won a
piece.

| 19 Kt—K4 ! | B × R |
| 20 Kt—Q6 ch | K—B1 |

Lasker recommends the simpler 20 . . . K—K2 !; 21 Kt
× R ch, R × Kt; 22 R × B, P—
Kt4 ! followed by . . . P—B3
with good winning chances.
But Bernstein apparently fears
the Bishops on opposite colors.

| 21 Kt × R | B—KKt4 |

Nimzovich has conjured up
some wonderful tactical possi-
bilities here in the variation 21
. . . B × P; 22 R—Q1 !:
I 22 . . . K—K1; 23 Kt—
Q6 ch, K—K2 (if 23 . . . K

[49

—B1; 24 Kt × QBP wins a
piece); 24 Kt × QBP, B—B6;
25 B—B5 *ch*, K—K1; 26 Kt—
Q6 *ch* winning at least a
piece!

II 22 . . . B × Kt; 23 R—
Q8 *ch*, K—K2; 24 R × R, K—
Q2 (if 24 . . . B—Q2 *?*; 25
B—B5 mate!); 25 R—Q8 *ch*,
K—B3; 26 R—Q6 *ch*, K—Kt4;
27 B—K3 *!!* and one of the
Bishops is lost! (Nimzovich).

III 22 . . . B—K1; 23 R
—Q8, P—B6; 24 B—B5 *ch*,
K—Kt1; 25 R × B *ch*, K—R2;
26 R × R *ch*, K × R; 27 B—
Q4 and wins (Lasker).

22 P—B4 *! ?*   B × Kt

Lasker shows a complicated
draw here with 22 . . . B × P;
23 R—Q1, K—K1 (not 23
. . . B—K1; 24 R—Q8, B ×
P *ch*; 25 K—B2, B × P; 26 B
—B5 *ch*, K—Kt1; 27 R × B
ch, K—R2; 28 R × R *ch*, K ×
R; 29 Kt—Q6 *!*, B × P; 30 Kt
× BP, B—B3; 31 Kt—Q6 and
should win); 24 Kt—Q6 *ch*,
K—K2; 25 B—B5, P—Kt3 *!*;
26 Kt—B5 *ch*, K—K1; 27 Kt
—Q6 *ch* etc.

23 P × B   B—Q2
24 R—Q1   K—K2

25 B—B5 *ch*   K—K1
26 R—Q4   B—B3

Superficial: Lasker gives 26
. . . R—R4 *!*; 27 P—KR4, P
—B3 with a likely draw.

27 R × P

Nimzovich's play in the remaining portion of the game is
described by the great Lasker
as "masterly" and "classic."
*White's winning chances de-
rive from his powerful hold on
the black squares.*

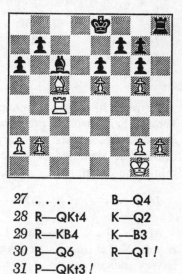

27 . . . .   B—Q4
28 R—QKt4   K—Q2
29 R—KB4   K—B3
30 B—Q6   R—Q1 *!*
31 P—QKt3 *!*

Bernstein had hoped for 31
R × P, when 31 . . . R—Q2

yields a drawn position. But Nimzovich has a subtle plan in view.

31	R—Q2
32 P—KR4 *!*	P—R4
33 P—KKt4 *!*	

A terrible menace appears for Black: White aims at a passed King Rook Pawn.

33 . . . .   P—Kt4

Perhaps he can liquidate the Queen-side?!

34 P—R5	P × P
35 P × P	P—R5
36 P × P	B × P

Gives White a new weapon; but if 36 . . . P × P; 37 B—B8 should win.

| 37 P—R5 *!* | R—R2 |
| 38 B—B8 | B—Kt8 |

If 38 . . . R × P; 39 R × P and wins.

39 R—B1	B—Q6
40 R—Q1	B—B4
41 B—Kt4 *!*	

He preserves the passed Pawn, which will soon be joined by a companion.

41 . . . .   R—R1

If 41 . . . R—Q2; 42 R—Q6 *ch!* leaves Black helpless.

| 42 R—Q6 *ch* | K—B2 |
| 43 P—QR6 *!* | R—R1 |

The threat was 44 B—R5 *ch,* K—Kt1; 45 R—Q8 *ch,* K—R2; 46 B—Kt6 *ch* etc.

44 B—B5 *!*   B—Kt5

But not 44 . . . R × P *? ?*; 45 B—Kt6 *ch* and mate next move. Thus the advance of the King's Rook Pawn has been provided for!

45 P—R6 *!*	P × P
46 P × P	K—Kt1
47 K—B2	B—B4

If 47 . . . R × P; 48 P—

R7 *ch* and the Pawn must queen.

48 K—B3	P—Kt5
49 B—K3	K—R1
50 R—Kt6	R—KB1
51 R × KtP	P—B3

Hoping to have some drawing chances by reduction of material. But Nimzovich concludes the game beautifully.

52 B—B5 !	R—B1

If 52 . . . R—B2 (or 52 . . . R—R1; 53 P × P, R × P; 54 P—B7); 53 R—Kt7 !, R ×

R; 54 P × R *ch,* K × P; 55 P × P and one of the Pawns must queen!

53 P × P !	R × B
54 P—B7	R—B1
55 R—Kt7 !	B—Q6

If 55 . . . B—Kt3; 56 R—K7, R—B1; 57 R—K8 *ch,* R × R; 58 P × R(Q) *ch,* B × Q; 59 P—KR7 wins!

56 R—K7	B—Kt4
57 K—B4 !	

But not 57 R—K8 ?, B × R ! (57 . . . R × R ? loses); 58 P—B8(Q), B—B3 *ch* and wins!

57	R—R1
58 P—KR7	B—R5
59 K—K5	B—Kt4
60 K—B6	P—K4
61 K—Kt7	Resigns

For all its imperfections, this exciting and witty game could have been played only by two great masters.

14.   *Means and Ends*

IN ALL human affairs, the great problem is to harmonize means with ends. In science, we must find the logical connecting link between millions of observed details and the great general laws which rule their functions. In chess, we must reconcile broad strategical concepts with myriads of subtle tactical finesses. In each case we are dealing with the conflict between the general and the particular.

Lord Bacon put the problem beautifully when he wrote in his *Novum Organum* more than 300 years ago: "Some minds are stronger and apter to mark the differences of things, others to mark their resemblances. The steady and acute mind can fix its contemplations and dwell and fasten on the subtlest distinctions; the lofty and discursive mind recognizes and puts together the finest and most general resemblances. Both kinds, however, easily err in excess, by catching the one at gradations, the other at shadows."

Nimzovich was one of the deepest thinkers in the history of chess: he founded a system based on general principles which could be applied to specific positions. Hence his tactical prowess was supported by the strength of generalized thought. An opponent like Freymann, relying on improvised tactics only, was bound to succumb. That is the moral of the following game.

FRENCH DEFENSE

Russian Championship—Vilna, 1912

WHITE: *A. Nimzovich*   BLACK: *S. von Freymann*

1 P—K4	P—K3	2 P—Q4	P—Q4

3 P—K5	P—QB4	12 P—KR3	Kt—B4
4 Kt—KB3	P × P	13 B—R2	
5 Kt × P			

Varying from the previous game, in which he played 5 Q × P.

The continuation 13 B × Kt *?*, P × B; 14 P—K6 *?* would obviously be bad for White: 14 . . . P—B5; 15 P × P *ch*, K × P etc.

5	Kt—QB3
6 Kt × Kt	P × Kt

13 . . . .   P—Kt5 *? !*

The issue has been drawn very sharply: Black relies on occupation of the center by Pawns (Classical theory), while White relies on occupation of the center by his pieces (Hypermodern theory).

"Brilliant," but it has the fatal *strategical* drawback of resigning control of White's KB4.

7 B—Q3	Q—B2
8 B—KB4	P—Kt4 *?*

This anti-positional advance gains time for further attack on the King's Pawn (if 9 B × KtP *?*, Q × P *ch* wins a piece), but it weakens the King-side badly. The more solid . . . Kt —K2—Kt3 was in order.

14 R—K1 *!*

9 B—Kt3	B—KKt2
10 Q—K2	Kt—K2
11 O—O	P—KR4

He overprotects the King Pawn instead of falling for 14 P × P, P × P; 15 Q × P *?*, R × B *!*; 16 K × R, B × P *ch* followed by 17 . . . B × P.

The logic of the situation calls for a continuation in coffee-house vein.

14 . . . .   K—B1

. . . P × P would be of no use to Black, since his inferior development makes a sustained attack impossible.

15 Kt—B3 !

Again Nimzovich tends his strategical fences: the Knight is headed for KB4. 15 P × P, P × P; 16 Q × P? is still answered by . . . R × B ! etc.

15 . . . .   Q—K2

So that if 16 P × P, P × P; 17 Q × P, R—R5 followed by 18 . . . Q—Kt4 with good attacking prospects.

16 B × Kt !   P × B

Black is left with an unwieldy King-side Pawn structure, easily blockaded by a White piece at KB4.

17 Q—K3   R—R3

Or 17 . . . B—KR3; 18 B —B4 with advantage to White.

18 Kt—K2 !   P—B4
19 Kt—B4 !   P—Q5

Inevitable. But Black's Pawns at Q5 and QB4 look stronger than they actually are.

20 Q—Q3   Q—Q2

If 20 . . . B—K3; 21 P— QB3 is a highly advantageous reply.

21 Q—B4   Q—B3

22 P × P !

If 22 Kt—Q3, P × P; 23 Q × QBP *ch*, Q × Q; 24 Kt × Q, R—KKt3; 25 P—KKt3 (Nimzovich) and White's Bishop is buried.

22 . . . .   B—R3

On 22 . . . BP × P; 23 Kt— Q3 Black loses a Pawn without the compensation of the open King Rook file. But the text is answered forcefully.

23 Q—Q5 !

[55

23 . . . .   Q × Q

If Black captures the Pawn either way, there follows 24 P—K6 *!!* (this Pawn should have been blockaded!), Q × Q; 25 P—K7 *ch !*, K—K1; 26 Kt × Q and wins!

24 Kt × Q   B—B5

Again, if the Pawn is captured, White wins with 25 P—K6 *!*, for example 25 . . . R × P; 26 R × R, P × R; 27 Kt—B7.

25 Kt—B6 *!*   RP × P

If 25 . . . B × Kt; 26 P × B, R × P; 27 B—K5 followed by 28 P × BP or 26 . . . RP × P; 27 B—Q6 *ch.*

26 B—B4   R—Kt3
27 Kt—Q7 *ch*   K—K2

28 Kt × P   R—QB1
29 P—Kt4   B—KR3

Hoping for 30 B × B *?*, R × B when . . . QR—KR1 is a troublesome threat.

30 QR—Q1 *!*   B × B
31 R × P   R—KR3
32 R × QB   QR—KR1
33 K—B1   R—R8 *ch*
34 K—K2   R × R *ch*
35 K × R   B × P
36 Kt—Q3

Nimzovich has parried the threat with artful simplification, and the game has reached a purely technical stage.

36 . . . .   B—Q3
37 P—R4   P—R4
38 P—Kt5   R—R8 *ch*
39 K—K2   R—R7
40 Kt—B4 *!*   B × Kt
41 R × B   R × P
42 P—B4   R—Kt8
43 R × BP   K—K3
44 R—Q5   R—Kt8
45 R—Q8   K—K2
46 R—QR8   R—Kt5
47 P—B5   R × RP
48 P—Kt6   R—Kt5
49 P—B6   R × P
50 P—B7   Resigns

15. *Forgotten*

SIMON ALAPIN, who was born in 1856 and lived well into the third decade of the twentieth century, had much in common with his younger compatriot Nimzovich. Alapin was a witty writer, an indefatigable polemicist, an original analyst and an eccentric and irascible man. He did valuable work on the theory of the openings, particularly in the French Defense and the early elaboration of the Slav Defense. The rarely encountered opening (1 P—K4, P—K4; 2 Kt—K2 ?) which has been named after him, is a monument to his crotchety avoidance of orthodoxy.

As a practical player, he achieved only mediocre results. In his youth he was overshadowed by the immortal Tchigorin; in later years, he was outdistanced by such younger Russian masters as Nimzovich, Alekhine, Rubinstein and Bernstein.

FRENCH DEFENSE

Riga, 1913

WHITE: *A. Nimzovich* BLACK: *S. Alapin*

1 P—K4	P—K3
2 P—Q4	P—Q4
3 Kt—QB3	

One of the few occasions on which Nimzovich does not play his favorite 3 P—K5.

3	Kt—KB3
4 P × P	Kt × P

Tarrasch would have criticized this move on the ground that Black gives up his foothold in the center; 4 ... P × P is the proper move for this purpose, but Alapin does not care for the rather arid possibilities of the Exchange Variation; besides, he has another way of clearing the center.

[57

| 5 Kt—B3 | P—QB4 |

This explains his previous move: he intends to achieve theoretical equality by eliminating White's center Pawn as well. While this plan is theoretically impeccable, it has tactical drawbacks, as Nimzovich will demonstrate; hence 5 . . . Kt × Kt; 6 P × Kt, P—QB4, with promising play against White's somewhat weakened Pawn structure, was called for.

| 6 Kt × Kt | Q × Kt |

Recapturing with the Pawn has the unsatisfactory feature of leading to an isolated Pawn.

7 B—K3 !   P × P

Thus he carries out his plan of liquidating White's Pawn

center, but at what a cost in development!

| 8 Kt × P | P—QR3 |

Another lost tempo, but he cannot allow a further improvement in White's position with 9 Kt—Kt5.

9 B—K2	Q × KtP ?
10 B—B3	Q—Kt3
11 Q—Q2	

Nimzovich's plan is simple: he intends to castle, after which he can deploy his Rooks on the center files which Black has so conveniently opened for him, or else he can operate on the King Knight file.

| 11 . . . . | P—K4 |

This leads to a crisis. Alapin sees that he cannot escape by castling, for example 11 . . . B—K2; 12 O—O—O, O—O; 13 KR—Kt1; Q—B3; 14 B—Kt5 and wins. Or 11 . . . B—B4; 12 O—O—O, O—O; 13 Kt—B6 !, Kt × Kt; 14 B × B, R—K1 (if 14 . . . R—Q1; 15 Q × R ch etc.); 15 B × Kt, P × B; 16 KR—Kt1, Q—B3; 17 B—Q4, P—K4; 18 B × P !, Q

× B; 19 either R—K1 and
wins.

Q—Q8 *ch*, Kt × Q; 16 R × Kt
mate.

12 O—O—O !

Nimzovich's advantage con-
sists in rapid development;
hence he increases it.

12 . . . .   P × Kt

Black should have tried 12
. . . Q—Q3; but he is rendered
desperate by the undeveloped
state of his Queen-side.

13 B × QP   Kt—B3

Else White plays 14 B ×
KKtP threatening Q—Q8
mate. If 13 . . . B—K2; 14 KR
—K1 will prove decisive.

14 B—B6 ! !

Beginning a magnificent
combination. The threat is 15

14 . . . .   Q × B

If 14 . . . P × B or . . . B
—K3 or . . . B—K2; 15 B ×
Kt *ch* forces a quick mate.
Now Black has swallowed two
pieces, but he soon chokes on
them.

15 KR—K1 *ch*   B—K2

If 15 . . . B—K3; 16 Q—Q7
mate.

16 B × Kt *ch*   K—B1

16 . . . Q × B allows 17 Q—
Q8 mate. If 16 . . . B—Q2;
17 Q × B *ch*, K—B1; 18 Q—
Q8 *ch* ! and mate follows.

17 Q—Q8 *ch* ! B × Q
18 R—K8 mate

[59

16. The Knights Work Wonders

NIMZOVICH was the virtuoso of blockading strategy and he was also an artist in the handling of the Knights. Since these pieces are the blockading forces *par excellence*, there is doubtless an inner connection between two such notable skills.

So great was Nimzovich's ability in these respects that he sometimes succeeded (as here and in Game 10), in holding at bay two hostile Bishops in an open position!

FRENCH DEFENSE

Russian Championship—St. Petersburg, 1914

WHITE: *A. Nimzovich*　　　BLACK: *S. von Freymann*

1 P—K4	P—K3
2 P—Q4	P—Q4
3 P—K5	P—QB4
4 Kt—KB3	P × P

From a rigorous theoretical standpoint, this must be viewed as an attempt to show that White's King Pawn is weak—a notion that proved costly to many of Nimzovich's opponents.

5 Q × P

In Game 14 against the same player, Nimzovich had tried the even more debonair 5 Kt × P.

5	Kt—QB3
6 Q—KB4	Q—B2
7 B—QKt5	

Doubtless an improvement on his 7 Kt—B3 against Bernstein in the same position (see Game 13).

7	Kt—K2
8 O—O	Kt—Kt3
9 Q—Kt3	B—Q2
10 R—K1	

Nimzovich's ingenuity in the handling of this variation always bordered on the miraculous (which explains why very few other players have suc-

ceeded in doing equally well with it!). Black cannot play to win the King's Pawn: 10 . . . KKt × P?; 11 Kt × Kt, Kt × Kt; 12 B × B *ch* winning a piece.

10 . . . .   **O—O—O**

Practically forced, as White is threatening P—KR4—5 very strongly.

11 B × Kt   P × B

Better 11 . . . B × B; the text allows White to open the Queen's Bishop file later on with powerful effect.

12 B—Kt5 *!*   R—K1
13 P—B4 *!*   P—B3 *? !*

White cannot very well accept his opponent's interesting Pawn sacrifice: 14 KP × P, B

—Q3 *!;* 15 Q—R3, P—K4; 16 Q—R5, KtP × P; 17 B × P, KR—B1; 18 B—Kt5, P—K5 with a beautiful attacking position. However, by declining the Greek gift, Nimzovich turns it to his own advantage! His principle of *blockade* is justified here if only by the fact that Black's attack is automatically smothered.

14 B—B4 *!*   B—Kt5
15 Kt—B3   KR—B1

Threatening 16 . . . Kt × B; 17 Q × Kt, BP × P; 18 Q × P, B—Q3 with a strong attack. The alternative 15 . . . B × Kt closes the Queen Bishop file, but opens the Queen Knight file for White.

16 BP × P *!*

[61

16 . . . .   KBP × P

17 . . . P × B was somewhat
better, but Black's King would
still be dangerously exposed.

18 B × P   Kt × B
19 Kt × Kt   B—B4

Black's Bishops look very
powerful, but Nimzovich tames
them easily enough!

20 R—K2   B—Kt2
21 Kt—Kt5   Q—Kt3
22 R—QB1 !

Combining attack and blockade very skilfully.

Against the crucial alterna-
tive 16 . . . KP × P Nimzovich
intended to proceed with 17
Kt × P !, P × Kt; 18 KR—B1,
B—B3; 19 Kt—Q4, Kt × B;
20 Q × Kt ! (20 R × B ?, Q
× R !; 21 Kt × Q, Kt—K7 ch),
P × P; 21 Q—Kt4 ch with a
winning game, for example 21
. . . Q—Q2; 22 R × B ch, K—
Q1; 23 Kt—K6 ch or 21 . . .
K—Kt2; 22 Kt × B, B—Q3
(if 22 . . . B—K2; 23 Q—K6 !);
23 Q—Q1 !, P—Q5; 24 Q—
Kt3 ch, K—R1; 25 Q—Q5 etc.

22 . . . .   Q × Kt
23 KR—B2   K—Kt1
24 R × B   R—B1

A last gasp; if instead 24
. . . Q—R3; 25 Kt—Q7 ch
wins easily.

25 Kt—Q3 ch Resigns

For now the Queen can be
captured. Typical Nimzovich
from the first move to the last:
sly, piquant and above all: "bizarre."

17 P × BP   B × P

17. *Riga and its Gambit*

SOME localities are notable for the unusual interest which they take in chess. The result is very often a favorable climate for the production of able players, analysts, problem and endgame composers. The Latvian city of Riga is one of the outstanding examples of this phenomenon: the names of Nimzovich, Behting, Sehwers, Mattison and Petrov, to mention no others, have given this chess-loving city great and honorable fame in the chess world.

In large part, Riga's chess reputation is based on the famous correspondence games which the Riga Chess Club contested successfully with some of the world's most famous, and larger, clubs. Skill at postal chess is often related to analytical ability. For years the players of Riga, led by Carl Behting, have devoted themselves, with some measure of success, to the rehabilitation of the venerable Greco Counter Gambit. In some quarters the defense has been renamed the Latvian Gambit, by way of tribute to their efforts.

GRECO COUNTER GAMBIT

Riga, 1919

WHITE: *A. Nimzovich*   BLACK: *C. Behting*

| 1 P—K4 | P—K4 |
| 2 Kt—KB3 | P—KB4 |

It is interesting to see how Nimzovich proceeds against this defense, of which he himself had a good opinion.

| 3 Kt × P | Q—B3 |

4 P—Q4	P—Q3
5 Kt—B4	P × P
6 Kt—K3	

A favorite move with Nimzovich, although 6 Kt—B3, Q —Kt3; 7 B—B4, Kt—KB3; 8

Kt—K3, B—K2; 9 B—B4, P
—B3; 10 P—Q5 (Thomas—
Tartakover, Spa, 1926) is clearly in White's favor. The text is
also good, but leads to more
complex play.

6 . . . .   P—B3

This proves unsatisfactory,
but the alternative course recommended by the Riga ana-
lysts (6 . . . Kt—B3; 7 P—Q5,
Kt—K4; 8 Kt—B3, Q—Kt3;
9 Q—Q4, Kt—KB3; 10 Kt—
Kt5, K—Q1) is not to everyone's taste.

7 B—B4 ! !

One of the famous Nimzo-
vich moves. It looks nonsensi-
cal, as the Bishop can be driv-
en away at once.

7 . . . .   P—Q4

8 B—Kt3   B—K3

He realizes that he cannot
ward off the following attack
on his Pawn chain with 8 . . .
P—QKt4 because of the powerful reply 9 P—QR4.

9 P—QB4 !

Suddenly highlighting the
weakness of Black's advanced
Pawns. Now we see why Nimzovich's weird-looking seventh
move was so strong.

9 . . . .   Q—B2
10 Q—K2   Kt—B3

So far so good; but he is destined to have trouble with the
Pawn structure for the rest of
the game.

11 O—O

The immediate 11 Kt—B3
is met by 11 . . . B—QKt5.

11 . . . .   B—QKt5

If 11 . . . QKt—Q2 or . . .
B—Q3; 12 P × P, P × P; 13
Kt—B3 (the excursion of the
White Queen to Kt5 is a good
alternative) and Black is in
serious difficulties.

12 B—Q2   B × B

13 Kt × B

16 P—B5

Not only does White have a strategical advantage: he is developing more rapidly.

13 . . . .   O—O

14 P—B4 !

A new menace. White threatens to win at least a Pawn with 15 P—KB5. If 14 . . . P × P e.p.; 15 Kt × BP, P —KR3 (not 15 . . . P × P; 16 Kt—Kt5); 16 P × P, P × P; 17 Kt—K5, Q—K1; 18 Kt—B5 with a winning position.

14 . . . .   P × QBP
15 Kt(2) × BP   Q—K2

If 15 . . . QKt—Q2; 16 Kt —Q6 wins the Queen's Knight Pawn.

16 . . . .   B—Q4

This soon leads to a catastrophe on the diagonal; however, if 16 . . . B—B2; 17 QR —K1 followed by P—Kt4 and Q—Kt2, after which the days of the King's Pawn are numbered.

17 Kt × B   P × Kt

Forced; if 17 . . . Kt × Kt; 18 Kt—K3, Q—Q3; 19 Kt × Kt, P × Kt; 20 Q × P and wins.

18 Kt—K3   Q—Q2
19 Kt × P !

The winning move. It is interesting that the final demolition of the weak center is only incidental to the combination.

[65

| 19 . . . . | Kt × Kt |
| 20 Q × P | R—Q1 |

21 P—B6 !

The advance of this Pawn, which has been longing to move up, is decisive. For instance, if 21 . . . P—KKt3; 22 P—B7 *ch*, K—B1; 23 Q—R4, K—Kt2; 24 B × Kt and wins.

Nimzovich points out that 21 . . . Kt—B3 is refuted by 22 P—B7 *ch*, K—R1 (if 22

. . . K—B1; 23 Q × P etc.); 23 B × Kt, Q × B; 24 P—B8(Q) *ch*, R × Q; 25 Q × Q etc.

21	P × P
22 R—B5	K—R1
23 R × Kt	R—K1

On 23 . . . Q—K1; 24 B—B2 *!* wins at least a Rook. Or 23 . . . Q—B1 and 24 Q—K7 is brutally decisive.

| 24 R × Q | R × Q |
| 25 R—Q8 *ch* | K—Kt2 |
| 26 R—Kt8 *ch !* |

Even stronger than R—QB1 —B8.

| 26 . . . . | K—R3 |
| 27 R—KB1 | Resigns |

Quite right. The demolition of Black's game was carried out with classic deftness.

18. *Nip and Tuck*

IN MODERN times, there has been much loose talk of a dearth of fighting chess between the great masters. This gossip, when there has been substance to it, was justified in the case of players whose judgment is more highly developed than their courage. But with natural fighters such as Nimzovich and Spielmann, an exciting struggle is always indicated.

FRENCH DEFENSE

Stockholm, 1920

WHITE: *A. Nimzovich*   BLACK: *R. Spielmann*

1	P—K4	P—K3
2	P—Q4	P—Q4
3	P—K5	P—QB4
4	Kt—KB3	Kt—QB3
5	P—B3	Q—Kt3
6	B—K2	P × P
7	P × P	Kt—R3

9	Kt—QR4	Q—R4 *ch*
10	B—Q2	B—Kt5
11	B—B3	

Regarding the opening play, see Game 12, in which Nimzovich was a tempo behind the present game by reason of his having played 6 B—Q3.

8 Kt—B3 *! ?*

Varying from the almost obligatory 8 P—QKt3.

8 . . . .   Kt—B4

White's task in guarding the base (Q4) of his Pawn-chain is not easy. For example, Black

[67

can now win a Pawn by 11
. . . B × B *ch*, on which Nim-
zovich gives 12 Kt × B, Q—
Kt3; 13 B—Kt5, O—O; 14
B × Kt, Q × KtP; 15 Kt—
QR4, Q—Kt5 *ch;* 16 Q—Q2
and the extra Pawn is worth-
less for winning purposes: the
White forces will be too strong-
ly entrenched on the Queen
Bishop file.

11	B—Q2
12 P—QR3	B × B *ch*
13 Kt × B	P—R4
14 O—O	QR—B1
15 Q—Q2	Q—Q1

Preparing for his next move:
the basic strategical problem is
a struggle for mastery of the
Queen Bishop file.

16 P—R3 *!*	Kt—R4

Nimzovich's subtle last move
has discouraged Black from
playing 16 . . . P—KKt4,
which is answered by 17 P—
KKt4, P × P; 18 P × P, Kt—
R5; 19 Kt × Kt, R × Kt; 20
K—Kt2 followed by 21 R—R1
and White has much the better
of it.

17 QR—Q1	Q—Kt3

18 KR—K1	Kt—B5
19 B × Kt	R × B

Both players are satisfied:
White has over-protected his
center Pawns, Black has temporary control of the Queen
Bishop file.

20 Kt—K2	B—R5
21 QR—B1	B—Kt6
22 R × R	B × R
23 Kt—Kt3	Kt—K2

After the exchange of
Knights, Black would become
weak on the black squares, and
his Bishop would be at a disadvantage against the remaining Knight.

24 P—KR4 *!*	Kt—Kt3
25 Kt—B1	B × Kt

Spielmann is delighted to
part with the Bishop; but now
he loses the open file.

26 R × B	Kt—K2
27 R—B1	O—O
28 P—QKt4	Kt—B4
29 R—B5	Q—R3 *!*
30 Q—B3	Q—K7

Black's position is difficult,
but Spielmann is defending
cleverly. The presence of the

Queen is inconvenient for White, and it is not clear how he is to make progress: 31 R—B7 leads to nothing because of 31 ... Q—R3, while 31 Q—B2 is answered by 31 ... Kt × QP!

31 Q—B2 !   Kt × QP !
32 Q × Q !

Not 32 Kt × Kt ?, Q—K8 ch; 33 K—R2, Q × P ch etc.

32 . . . .   Kt × Q ch
33 K—B1   Kt—B5

Now we see the point of Nimzovich's profound sacrifice: White's Rook reaches the seventh rank. But thanks to his passed Pawn, Black's position is capable of stubborn resistance.

34 R—B7   P—QKt4 ?

Passive resistance by 34 ... R—Kt1 has little to offer because of 35 Kt—Kt5 etc., but 34 ... P—QKt3 would have gained valuable time.

35 P—Kt3   Kt—Q6
36 K—K2   Kt—Kt7
37 R × RP   R—B1

Recovering the open file, Spielmann counters vigorously; it requires all of Nimzovich's skill to press his advantage.

38 Kt—Q4   R—B5
39 Kt × KtP   P—Q5

Relying on the passed Pawn; the more aggressive 39 ... R—B7 ch; 40 K—B1, Kt—Q6; 41 P—B4, P—Kt4 ! ?; 42 RP × P, P—R5 ! ?; 43 P × P, R—B7 ch; 44 K—Kt1, R × P is met by 45 Kt—Q6, 46 P—Kt5 etc.

40 R—B7 !   P—Q6 ch
41 K—K3   R—Kt5
42 R—B1   P—Kt4 !
43 Kt—Q6 !   P × P
44 P × P   R × RP
45 R—Kt1   R—R6 ch

[69

46 K—Q2   Kt—R5

Despite Spielmann's excellent defense, White's Queen Knight Pawn can at last advance.

47 P—Kt5   Kt—Kt3
48 R—Kt4 *!*

Much more exact than 48 P—R4, Kt × P; 49 P—Kt6, Kt × P; 50 R × Kt, R—B6 when White's winning prospects have dwindled considerably.

48 . . . .   R—B6 *!*
49 Kt—B4 *!*

The blockader must go!

49 . . . .   Kt—Q2

On 49 . . . Kt × Kt *ch;* 50

R × Kt, R × P *ch;* 51 K × P, R—B6 *ch* Nimzovich intended 52 K—B2, R × P; 53 R—B8 *ch !,* K—Kt2; 54 P—Kt6, R—R7 *ch;* 55 K—B3, R—R6 *ch;* 56 K—B4, R—R5 *ch;* 57 K—Kt5 and wins.

50 P—Kt6   Kt—B4 *!*

Although the Knight is condemned, Spielmann still manages to get some work out of him.

51 P—Kt7   R × P *ch*
52 K—K3   R—K7 *ch*
53 K—Q4   Kt × P
54 K × P *!*   R—KKt7
55 R × Kt   P—R5
56 Kt—K3   R—Kt4
57 K—Q4   P—R6
58 R—Kt2   R—R4
59 R—KR2   P—B3
60 Kt—B4   K—B2
61 P—R4   Resigns

On 61 . . . K—Kt3 Nimzovich planned 62 P—R5, P × P *ch;* 63 K—B5, K—B4; 64 P—R6, R—R2; 65 K—Kt6, K—Kt5; 66 Kt—K3 *ch !,* K—Kt6; 67 Kt—B1 *ch* (just in time!). One of Nimzovich's best endings.

19. *Greek Meets Greek*

IT IS always fascinating to see how a player reacts when he is called upon to play against one of his own favorite opening lines. Both Nimzovich and Marco were fond of the Hanham Variation of Philidor's Defense; so that Marco must have felt that he was setting Nimzovich a very searching test. Nimzovich's reaction is startling!

PHILIDOR'S DEFENSE

Gothenburg, 1920

WHITE: *A. Nimzovich*   BLACK: *G. Marco*

1	P—K4	P—K4
2	Kt—KB3	P—Q3
3	P—Q4	Kt—Q2

The once fashionable 3 . . . Kt—KB3 can be answered strongly by 4 P × P, Kt × P; 5 Q—Q5, Kt—B4; 6 B—Kt5 etc.

4	B—QB4	P—QB3

Black must play carefully in this trappy line. After the plausible 4 . . . B—K2 ?; 5 P × P wins a Pawn no matter how Black replies.

5 P—QR4

Restraining the expansion of

Black's Queen-side (see Game 7) by . . . P—QKt4 etc.

5	. . . .	B—K2
6	Kt—B3	KKt—B3
7	O—O	P—KR3

A wrinkle introduced by Breyer. The idea is to play

. . . Q—B2 followed by . . . Kt—B1—Kt3 (possibly preceded by . . . P—KKt4), and eventually . . . O—O—O with attacking chances.

How should this plan be met? Nimzovich's solution is startlingly original!

8 P—QKt3 !

Putting more pressure on the center: the basic conception is *strategic*, the means *combinative*.

| 8 . . . . | Q—B2 |
| 9 B—Kt2 | Kt—B1 ? |

9 . . . O—O was in order, although Black's game would remain cramped.

| 10 P × P | P × P |
| 11 Kt × P ! | Q × Kt ? |

Relatively best was 11 . . . Kt—K3, although after 12 P —B4 Black would have no better objective than losing as slowly as possible.

12 Kt—Q5 ! !

The brilliant second sacrifice reveals the depth of Nimzovich's plan.

| 12 . . . . | Q—Q3 |

What else? If 12 . . . Q— Kt1 (not 12 . . . Q × B ? ?; 13 Kt—B7 mate!); 13 Kt × B and Black's position is shattered (he cannot play 13 . . . K × Kt because of 14 B—R3 *ch*, K— K1; 15 B—Q6 checkmating the Queen!—just the sort of humorous touch one expects from Nimzovich).

13 B—R3 !

Always the best. The tempting 13 P—K5 is met by . . . Q × Kt, after which Black, with three minor pieces for the Queen, can keep his head above water for a while.

| 13 . . . . | P × Kt |

He has no choice: 13 . . .

P—B4 is answered by 14 P—
K5, Q × P; 15 R—K1, Kt—
K5; 16 R × Kt, Q × KR; 17
Kt—B7 mate.

14 B × Q	P × B
15 B × B	K × B
16 P—K5	

Black has managed to obtain three pieces for the Queen in this variation as well; but his King is insecure, his pieces tied up, and White is two Pawns to the good.

16	Kt(3)—Q2

If 16 . . . Kt—K1; 17 Q—Q5 follows with paralyzing effect.

17 Q—Q6 *ch*	K—Q1
18 P—B4 *!*	P—QR4

To bring out the Queen's Rook. On 18 . . . Kt—Kt3 *?* White wins a piece with 19 P—K6 *!*, P × KP; 20 P—B5 *!* etc.

19 P—B5	R—R3
20 Q—Q5	K—K2
21 Q × BP	R—QB3
22 Q—Q5	P—R4

Now the other Rook comes out: a pathetic situation.

23 Q × P	KR—R3
24 QR—K1	P—QKt3
25 Q—Q2	K—Q1
26 Q—Q5	R × P

A last try for a swindle.

27 P—K6	P × P
28 P × P	Kt × P
29 R × Kt	B—Kt2

Truly hope springs eternal.

30 R—B8 *ch !*	Resigns

It is mate next move.

20. Pas de Deux

IN GAMES between two great tacticians, there is sometimes a delightful series of surprise moves and equally surprising rejoinders. One is reminded of the increasingly intricate variations in *The Bluebird* ballet, in which each dancer tries to surpass the other in virtuosity. Such a contest requires showmanship—a quality which Nimzovich never lacked.

FRENCH DEFENSE

Match, 1920

WHITE: *A. Nimzovich*   BLACK: *E. Bogolyubov*

1 P—K4	P—K3
2 P—Q4	P—Q4
3 P—K5	P—QB4
4 Kt—KB3	Kt—QB3
5 P × P	B × P
6 B—Q3	P—B3

Black plays dogmatically to clear the center squares, hoping to enforce . . . P—K4 later on. The plan proves much too ambitious.

Inviting complications. After 6 . . . KKt—K2 Nimzovich would doubtless have sacrificed a Pawn by the speculative B—KB4 *! ?* If instead 7 O —O, Kt—Kt3 virtually forces 8 B × Kt with a good game for Black; 8 R—K1, Q—B2; 9 Q—K2, Kt—Q5 *!* is even more favorable for him.

8 Kt × P	Kt × Kt
9 Q × Kt	Kt—B3

7 Q—K2   P × P

74]

The Pawn position is reminiscent of similar situations in Games 10 and 11. As in the earlier games, Nimzovich convincingly demonstrates the value of controlling K5.

10 B—Kt5 *ch !* K—B2

He cannot play 10 . . . B—Q2 *?* because of 11 Q × P *ch.* After the text, Black threatens . . . B × P *ch.*

11 O—O   Q—Kt3

Apparently seizing the initiative, for he attacks the King Bishop and again threatens . . . B × P *ch.* The indicated 12 Q—K2 is bad because of 12 . . . P—K4 *!* followed by . . . B—KKt5 with a winning game. Has Nimzovich been outgeneraled?

12 Kt—B3 *!*   B × P *ch ? !*

The risk involved in this move (opening the King's Bishop file for White) outweighs any returns which Black can reasonably expect. Of course, if now 13 R × B *?*, Q × R *ch* etc.

13 K—R1   R—B1

Intending artificial castling with . . . K—Kt1; but he never gets that far.

14 Q—K2   B—Q5
15 Kt—R4 *!*   Q—B2
16 B—KB4 *! !*

If 16 Q—Q3, B—K4; 17 Q × RP, B—Q2 and Black has the initiative.

16 . . . .   P—K4
17 B—Kt3

Black seems to have succeeded in carrying out his plan: he has advanced the King's Pawn and White's pieces on the Queen-side are out of play. But Nimzovich's plans are much deeper. To begin with, he threatens 18 P—B3, smashing up Black's proud center.

17 . . . .   P—QR3
18 B—Q3   Q—Q2

This seems to be decisive, as he threatens to win a piece by . . . Q × Kt or . . . P—K5. Tartakover shows that 18 . . . P—QKt4 fails because of 19 P—B3, B—R2; 20 B × KP, Q—K2; 21 B × RP *!*, P × Kt;

[75

22 Q—R5 *ch*, K—K3; 23 B ×
Kt and wins.

19 B × KP *! !* Q × Kt

The crisis of the combination: if 19 . . . B × B; 20 Kt—
Kt6, Q—Q3; 21 Kt × R, B—
Q5; 22 QR—K1, B—Q2; 23
R × Kt *ch !*, K × R (if 22 . . .
P × R; 23 Q—R5 *ch* and mate
next move. If 23 . . . Q × R;
24 Q—R5 *ch*, P—Kt3; 25 Q
× RP *ch*, Q—Kt2; 26 B × P
ch wins); 24 R—B1 *ch*, K
—Kt4; 25 Q—Q2 *ch*, K—R5
(or 25 . . . K—R4; 26 B—
K2 *ch* and wins); 26 P—
Kt3 *ch*, K—R6; 27 Q—Kt5 *! !*
(more conclusive than 27 Q—
Kt2 *ch*, which also wins), Q—

R3 (what else?); 28 Q × Q *ch*,
P × Q; 29 R × R and wins.

Another complicated line is
21 . . . K—Kt1; 22 QR—K1,
R—K1 (if 22 . . . B—Q5; 23
P—B3, B—R2; 24 Q—K7 and
wins, for example 24 . . . Q—
B3; 25 Kt—B7, R—B2; 26 B
× P *ch !*); 23 Q—B2 *! !*, P—
Q5; 24 B—B5 *! !* and wins.

20 R—B4   B—Kt5

If 20 . . . R—K1; 21 Q—
R5 *ch* wins easily.

21 Q × B *!*   B × B *? !*

Hoping for 22 R × Q, Kt ×
Q etc.

22 R × Kt *ch !* Resigns

21. *Steinitz and Nimzovich*

WHEN Irving Chernev and the present writer were preparing *Chess Strategy and Tactics*, we were struck by the resemblance between Steinitz and Nimzovich: similar in temperament and technique, they met with much the same reception.

"Both of them preferred cramped positions and difficult defensive games requiring superhuman skill (rather than open positions and ready-made attacks); they formulated definite and highly integrated theories of the game; they were always inventing new moves, introducing new ideas, innovating, seeking the ultimate—all this making them tragically incomprehensible to their contemporaries. Their moves were almost invariably characterized as 'bizarre,' 'mysterious,' 'typically Steinitzian,' 'just the sort of move that Nimzovich likes to play,' etc., etc., etc."

NIMZOVICH DEFENSE

Stockholm, 1921

WHITE: *Wendel*

BLACK: *A. Nimzovich*

1 P—K4	Kt—QB3	5 B—KB4	Kt—Kt3
2 P—Q4	P—Q4	6 B—Kt3	P—QR3 *!*
3 Kt—QB3	P × P		

The acceptance of the gambit gives Black a difficult game; hence Nimzovich often resorted to the solid but cramping 3 . . . P—K3.

4 P—Q5   Kt—K4

This strange-looking move is useful later on.

7 P—B3   P—KB4 *!*

Apparently butchering his Pawn position, but Nimzovich knows what he is about: if now

8 P—KR4, P—K4 *!;* 9 P—R5,
Q—Kt4 *!* with a good game.

8 P × P	P—B5 *!*
9 B—B2	P—K4
10 Kt—B3	B—Q3
11 P—KR4	

Leads to nothing. Development with 11 B—Q3 etc. was indicated.

11	P—Kt4 *!*
12 P—R5	Kt—B1
13 B—R4	Q—Q2

Black's play is weird indeed!

14 B—K2   P—Kt5 *!*

Gaining ground on the Queen's wing. Note that he avoids 14 . . . Q—Kt5 *?;* 15 Kt × KP *!,* Q × KtP *? ?;* 16 B —B3 and the Queen is lost.

15 Kt—QKt1	Kt—B3 *!*

Forcing the following exchange, which opens the King Knight file for Black.

16 B × Kt	P × B
17 QKt—Q2	Q—Kt2

Black's plan is now clear. His King will remain in the center (echo of Steinitz!) while he operates simultaneously on both wings.

18 K—B1	Kt—Q2
19 P—R6	Q—Kt6 *!*
20 R—R3	Q—Kt1
21 Kt—R4	Kt—B4
22 R—R1	R—Kt1
23 P—B3	

The opening of the Queen Knight file will be brilliantly exploited by Nimzovich later on.

23	P × P
24 P × P	Q—Kt6
25 Q—B2	R—Kt1

White's game has become very difficult. Thus if 26 R— QKt1, R × R *ch;* 27 Kt × R, Q—K6; 28 Kt—Q2 (or 28 B —B3, B—Q2 with a winning

attack), R—Kt6; 29 P—B4, B —Q2; 30 R—R2 (if 30 KKt— B3, R × P; 31 K × R, Q × B *ch;* 32 K—Kt1, Kt—Q6; 33 R—R2, B—B4 *ch;* 34 K—R1, Kt—B7 *ch;* 35 R × Kt, Q × R and wins, or 30 Kt—B5, B × Kt; 31 P × B, P—K5 etc.), B — R5; 31 Q—B1, Kt—Q6; 32 B × Kt, B—B4; 33 Q—K1, Q —Kt8 *ch* and mate next move (*Chess Strategy and Tactics*).

26	Kt—B4	B—Q2
27	Kt × B *ch*	P × Kt
28	B—B3	B—Kt4 *ch*

Beginning the final combination.

The sacrifices which follow are in keeping with this remarkably original game. The force of Nimzovich's combination does not become fully apparent until his 39th move.

29 P—B4

If 29 K—Kt1, B—Q6 and wins; or 29 B—K2, Kt—Q6; 30 B—R5 *ch,* K—Q2; 31 K— Kt1, Q—K6 *ch;* 32 K—R2, Kt —B7; 33 Kt—B5, R × P *ch;* 34 K × R, R—Kt1 *ch;* 35 Kt —Kt7, Q—Kt6 mate.

29	. . . .	B × P *ch !*
30	Q × B	R—Kt7
31	B—K2	R—KKt5 *!*

Anticipating 32 R—R3, R × Kt; 33 R × Q, R—R8 *ch;* 34 K —B2, P × R *ch;* 35 K × P, R × R and wins.

32	Q—B1	R × Kt *!*
33	R × R	R × B *!*
34	K × R	Q × P *ch!*
35	K—Q1	Q—B8 *ch*

Forcing White's reply, for if

36 K—B2, Q—Q6 *ch;* 37 K—Kt2, Kt—R5 mate.

36 K—Q2	Q—Q6 *ch*
37 K—K1	Q—Kt6 *ch*
38 K—B1	Q × R
39 K—Kt1	Q—Kt6 *ch*

White has no chance. His defeat is only a matter of time.

40 K—R1	Q—R6 *ch*
41 K—Kt1	Kt × P
42 Q—B6 *ch*	K—B2

43 Q—B7 *ch*	K—Kt3
44 Q—Kt7 *ch*	K—R4
45 Q—Kt2	Q—K6 *ch*
46 K—R2	Kt—B7 !
47 R—KB1	Kt—Kt5 *ch*
48 K—R1	P—K5
49 R—KKt1	P—B4
50 P—R4	K × P
51 P—R5	K—Kt4
52 R—Kt1	P—B6
53 Q—Kt2	P—B7
Resigns	

22. *Another Immortal Game*

NIMZOVICH's blockading technique was sure death for unwary or inexperienced opponents. The moral of this game is that blockade attempts must be scotched at the first opportunity. The longer resistance is delayed, the more difficult it becomes.

FRENCH DEFENSE

Match, 1922

WHITE: *A. Nimzovich*   **BLACK:** *A. Hakansson*

1 P—K4	P—K3
2 P—Q4	P—Q4
3 P—K5	P—QB4
4 Q—Kt4 *?!*	

Nimzovich's favorite continuation after some unfavorable post-war experiences with 4 Kt—KB3, Kt—QB3; 5 P—B3.

The early development of the Queen has a "coffee-house" look about it, but the intention, according to Nimzovich, is to hamper Black's development. The presence of the Queen hinders the Black King Bishop from becoming active; White's King Pawn acts as a wedge preventing . . . Kt—KB3. In this scheme of things, the possible loss of the Queen's Pawn is a matter of indifference to White.

4	P × P
5 Kt—KB3	Kt—QB3
6 B—Q3	P—B4 ?

A mistake on several counts: it renders the King's Pawn backward, it does not resist the blockade, it robs Black of the important resource . . . P—B3.

Correct is 6 . . . Q—B2 *!;* 7 B—KB4 (if 7 Q—Kt3, P—B3 *!*), KKt—K2 followed by . . . Kt—Kt3 with a good game.

7 Q—Kt3	KKt—K2
8 O—O	Kt—Kt3
9 P—KR4 *!*	

Very unpleasant: the intention is to drive back the Knight, which has just arrived puffing and panting at Kt3.

9	Q—B2
10 R—K1	B—Q2
11 P—R3	O—O—O

In his panicky anxiety to get his King into safety, Black is willing to put up with the loss of the exchange resulting from 12 P—R5, KKt—K2; 13 Kt—Kt5, R—K1; 14 Kt—B7, R—Kt1; 15 Kt—Q6 *ch.* But Nimzovich prefers to continue his attacking maneuvers rather than stoop to low material gain.

12 P—Kt4	P—QR3 ?

Creating a target for a later Pawn-storming attack. Relatively better was 12 . . . K—Kt1, although White would

have a fine game after 13 B—
Kt2 etc.

13 P—R5   KKt—K2

The future of Black's King
Bishop looks black indeed!

14 B—Q2

In order to prepare for P—
R4 by guarding the Queen's
Knight Pawn. The see-saw
from one wing to the other is
agonizing for Black.

14 . . . .   P—R3
15 P—R4   P—KKt4
16 P—Kt5   P—B5
17 Q—Kt4   Kt—QKt1
18 P—B3 *!*   R—K1

Preparing the King's escape.

19 BP × P   K—Q1

Just in time, but too late
anyway!

20 R—QB1   Q—Kt3
21 P—R5   Q—R2
22 P—Kt6   Q—R1

Who else but Nimzovich
could have conjured up the
position of Black's Queen?!!

23 R—B7   Kt—B4
24 Kt—B3   B—K2
25 Kt × QP *!*   Kt × P

This combination leads to a
fine finish—by White.

26 Kt × Kt   P × Kt

27 Q × B *ch !*   Kt × Q
28 Kt—K6 mate

A playful conclusion.

23. *Inside Job*

HERE again we have the same situation as in Game 19. Nimzovich, the inventor of the Queen's Indian Defense, is called upon to play against it, with Saemisch, one of its warmest advocates, handling the Black pieces. With his intimate knowledge of the fine points of this subtle opening, Nimzovich proves himself the better player.

QUEEN'S INDIAN DEFENSE

Copenhagen, 1923

WHITE: *A. Nimzovich*   BLACK: *F. Saemisch*

1	P—Q4	Kt—KB3
2	P—QB4	P—K3
3	Kt—KB3	P—QKt3
4	P—KKt3	B—Kt2
5	B—Kt2	B—K2
6	O—O	O—O
7	Kt—B3	P—Q4

7 . . . Kt—K5 gives simpler equalizing possibilities.

8	Kt—K5	Q—B1

. . . P—B3 is preferable.

9	P × P	Kt × P
10	Kt × Kt	B × Kt
11	P—K4	

Nimzovich remarks that 11 B × B, P × B; 12 B—K3, Q—

K3; 13 Kt—Q3, Kt—Q2; 14 R—B1 (with strong pressure on the Queen's wing) is more straightforward.

11	. . . .	B—Kt2
12	Q—R4	

A good alternative is 12 B—K3 followed by R—B1. After the text, Black's struggle to free himself taxes the energies of both players.

12	. . . .	P—QB4
13	P—Q5 !	P—QKt4 !

Apparently achieving freedom, for if 14 Q × KtP, B—R3 wins the exchange.

14	Q—Kt3	P × P

[83

15 P × P   B—Q3

Black has made progress: his Queen-side majority of Pawns looks formidable, and he is blockading the passed Pawn. White's task: to neutralize the hostile Pawns and remove the hostile blockader.

16 B—B4 !

Offering a piece.

16 . . . .   Q—B2

Commendable prudence. On 16 . . . P—Kt4 Nimzovich intended 17 Kt × P, B × B; 18 Kt—R6 ch, K—Kt2; 19 P × B, K × Kt; 20 P × P ch, K—Kt2 (if 20 . . . K × P; 21 K—R1 ! followed by 22 R—KKt1 and Black can hardly hope to parry the attack on his ex-

84]

posed King); 21 Q—B3 ch, K—Kt1; 22 B—R3, Q—Q1; 23 B—K6 ch, R—B2; 24 P—B4 with a winning attack.

17 Kt—Q3 !   P—QR3

17 . . . P—B5 only loses a Pawn: 18 B × B, Q × B; 19 Q × KtP, B—R3; 20 Q—B5 !

18 P—QR4 ! !   P—B5

After 18 . . . P—Kt5; 19 KR—B1 Black has a lost game. He must therefore permit the opening of the Queen Rook file. At this point, however, he seems to be winning a piece!

19 Q—R3 !   B × B

Not 19 . . . B × Q; 20 B × Q, B—K2; 21 P—Q6, B × B; 22 P × B ! and wins. The text has the drawback of removing the blockader at Black's Q3, but if 19 . . . R—Q1; 20 KR—K1 !, K—B1; 21 B × B ch, R × B; 22 Kt—B5 !, B × P; 23 B × B, R × B; 24 Kt—Q7 ch, K—Kt1; 25 R—K8 mate.

20 Kt × B   Kt—Q2
21 P × P   P × P
22 Q—K7 !

22 . . . .   Q—Q1

Nimzovich's painstakingly formed plans are coming to fruition. White's Queen cannot be permitted to remain at the dominating post K7, but how to drive her away? If 22 . . . QR—K1; 23 Q—Kt4, Q—Kt3; 24 R—R5 and Black's game is untenable. Or 22 . . . KR—K1; 23 R × R, R × R; 24 P—Q6, Q—B1; 25 B—R3, B—B3; 26 R—K1 and White's pressure will be decisive.

23 P—Q6   B × B
24 K × B   Kt— B3

Not 24 . . . Q × Q; 25 P × Q, KR—K1; 26 R × R, R × R; 27 R—Q1 and wins.

25 KR—Q1   R × R

Now or never: if 25 . . . R—K1; 26 Q—B7 with decisive positional advantage.

26 R × R   Q × Q
27 P × Q   R—K1
28 R—R7   P—Kt4

Finally managing to remove the deadly Pawn; but the coming endgame is won for White.

29 Kt—K2 !   Kt—Q4
30 Kt—Q4   Kt × P

If 30 . . . R × P P; 31 R—R8 *ch* wins the exchange.

31 Kt × P   Kt—B3

Black's tenacity is of no avail: if 31 . . . R—Kt1; 32 Kt—Q6 wins.

32 Kt—Q6 !   Kt × R

32 . . . R—Kt1; 33 R—Kt7 leads to much the same kind of play.

33 Kt × R   Kt—Kt4

Nimzovich now demonstrates impressively that the superior position of his pieces and his preferable Pawn structure guarantee victory. The coming ending is one of his best.

[85

34 Kt—B6 *ch*   K—Kt2
35 Kt—Q5 *!*   P—B3
36 K—B3   K—B2
37 Kt—B3 *!*   Kt—Q5 *ch*

Exchanging Knights costs the Queen Bishop Pawn.

38 K—K4   Kt—Kt6
39 K—Q5   Kt—Q7
40 P—R3   P—B4
41 Kt—Q1 *!*   K—B3

If 41 . . . P—B5; 42 P × P, P × P; 43 K—Q4 followed by K—B3 and wins.

42 Kt—K3   Kt—K5
43 Kt × QBP   Kt × BP
44 P—QKt4   K—K2

Wearily trekking toward the new passed Pawn; but this one is implacable.

45 P—Kt5   K—Q2
46 P—Kt6   Kt—K5

Just in time: the threat was 47 Kt—K5 *ch*, K—B1; 48 K—B6 forcing the queening of the Pawn.

47 Kt—K5 *ch*   K—B1
48 K—B6   Kt—B3
49 Kt—Q3 *!*   Kt—Q2

This time White threatened 50 Kt—B5 followed by 51 P—Kt7 *ch*, K—Kt1; 52 Kt—R6 *ch* etc.

50 P—Kt7 *ch*   K—Q1
51 K—Q6   Kt—Kt1
52 Kt—Kt4 *!*   Kt—Q2
53 Kt—B6 *ch*   K—K1
54 K—B7 *!*   Resigns

For if 54 . . . P—B5; 55 Kt —K5 *!* etc. A true master game, finely played by Nimzovich and stubbornly defended by Saemisch.

24. New Wine in Old Bottles

SUCH innovators as Steinitz, Nimzovich and Breyer have put chess theory through so many violent changes that most chess players lag behind these far-reaching transformations. The concept of brilliancy, for example, needs to be brought up to date. Anderssen, Morphy and their disciples were able to smash their opponents with a minimum of effort; in later years, when defensive play had greatly improved, it became necessary to apply constriction technique against stubborn opponents.

With the passing years, constriction technique became wonderfully refined; it also deteriorated, very frequently, into sterile wood-shifting which rightly irritated the average chess player. One of Nimzovich's greatest contributions was the eternal freshness with which he treated this theme: the homely recipe was always garnished with piquant details.

QUEEN'S INDIAN DEFENSE

Copenhagen, 1923

WHITE: *F. Saemisch*   BLACK: *A. Nimzovich*

1	P—Q4	Kt—KB3
2	P—QB4	P—K3
3	Kt—KB3	P—QKt3
4	P—KKt3	B—Kt2

This whole defensive system, with its many ramifications, owes its existence to Nimzovich.

5	B—Kt2	B—K2

6	Kt—B3	O—O
7	O—O	P—Q4

This move is curiously counter to the whole body of Nimzovichian theory of the center. The consistent move would be 7 ... Kt—K5, operating in the center with the *pieces;* instead, Nimzovich uses the good old

[87

classical method of occupying
the center with a *Pawn*.

8 Kt—K5   P—B3

At once neutralizing the
pressure on the long diagonal
and unpinning his Queen's
Bishop—at the cost, to be sure,
of obtaining rather a cramped
position.

9 P × P

Too easy-going. Best is the
energetic advance 9 P—K4!
with a promising game.

9 . . . .   BP × P

The Pawn exchange has
eased Black's game considerably. Nimzovich soon begins
to utilize hidden assets in an
unexpected manner.

10 B—B4   P—QR3!

Beginning an expansion maneuver on the Queen-side
which gains valuable space for
Black's pieces. 11 P—QR4
would prevent Black's next
move, but it would only weak-
en White's Queen-side without essentially hampering Nimzovich's plans.

11 R—B1   P—QKt4
12 Q—Kt3   Kt—B3
13 Kt × Kt

This looks uninspired, but
after 14 KR—Q1, Kt—QR4
followed by . . . Kt—B5 Black
has the initiative on the Queen-
side.

13 . . . .   B × Kt

Thus Black has disposed of
his opponent's well placed
Knight. Saemisch seems puzzled for a continuation, judg-
ing from his next two moves.

14 P—KR3   Q—Q2!

This prevents Kt—R4 in
reply to a future . . . P—Kt5.
The constriction process is
slowly taking shape.

15 K—R2   Kt—R4!

16 B—Q2   P—B4 *!*

Now Nimzovich has a strong game on both wings. He can either continue with . . . B—Q3 and . . . P—B5 or with . . . Kt—B3, . . . P—Kt5 and . . . Kt—K5. And since White cannot play P—K4, his prospects have become rather slim.

17 Q—Q1   P—Kt5
18 Kt—Kt1   B—QKt4 *!*

Improving his position and at the same time preventing P—K4.

19 R—Kt1   B—Q3 *!!*

Beginning a wonderfully subtle combination. He allows P—K4—but at a price.

20 P—K4   BP × P *!*
21 Q × Kt   R × P

Black has only two Pawns for the piece, but further instalments are due: his control of the seventh rank, the King Bishop file and two important diagonals are more valuable than mere material.

22 Q—Kt5

If 22 Q—Q1, QR—KB1 threatening 23 . . . QR—B6 or 23 . . . B × P *ch* or 23 . . . Q—K2 followed by 24 . . . Q—R5.

22 . . . .   QR—KB1

Threatening 23 . . . R(1)—B6; 24 B—B4, R × B *!*; 25 P × R, B × P *ch* etc. with an easy win. The helplessness of White's forces is quite striking.

23 K—R1   R(1)—B4 *!*
24 Q—K3   B—Q6 *!*

Threatening to win the Queen with 25 . . . R—K7.

25 QR—K1   P—R3 *!!*

A fantastic winning move. White resigns!

[89

With so many pieces still on the board, White finds himself in *Zugzwang!* Moves of his Queen-side Pawns don't count,

and the other possibilities are disposed of as follows: (a) 26 B—QB1, B × Kt regaining the piece with an easy win; (b) 26 R—Q1, R—K7 winning the Queen; (c) 26 B—KB1, R(4)—B6 *!* winning the Queen—this explains Black's peculiar 25th move; (d) 26 K—R2, R(4)—B6 again winning the Queen; (e) 26 P—Kt4, R(4)—B6; 27 B × R, R—R7 mate.

It is a far cry from Anderssen's "Immortal Games" to this "Immortal *Zugzwang* Game."

25. Optimism

IN THE last resort," Nimzovich writes somewhere in *My System*, "optimism is decisive in chess. I mean by this that it is psychologically valuable to develop to the greatest length the faculty of being able to rejoice over small advantages." Nimzovich even pushed this faculty one step further: he rejoiced over advantages which were so small that his opponents did not realize that the advantages were there.

Of course, optimism can be very risky—the Bogolyubov brand of optimism which we encounter, for example, in Games 43 and 49. The famous philosopher William James held that confidence helps one to perform a difficult task, but like all generalizations, the statement can be dangerous as well as useful. What matters in the last analysis, is an individual's specific intelligence, judgment and intuitive flair. Nimzovich had these necessary qualities.

QUEEN'S GAMBIT DECLINED

Carlsbad, 1923
(Second Brilliancy Prize)

WHITE: *A. Nimzovich*   BLACK: *J. Bernstein*

1	Kt—KB3	Kt—KB3
2	P—Q4	P—Q4
3	P—B4	P—K3
4	Kt—B3	B—K2
5	P—K3	O—O

Either here or on the next move, . . . P—B4 equalizes.

6	P—QR3	P—QR3

Not very much to the point, as White's reply shows.

7	P—B5	P—B3

White's attempt to constrict his opponent's game by P—B5 has created two Pawn-chains: White Pawns at Q4 and QB5, Black Pawns at QB3 and Q4. White contemplates attack on the base of the hostile Pawn-chain by an eventual P—QKt4—5; Black intends the same process by way of . . . P—K4.

Thus the coming strategy for both sides is clearly outlined.

8	P—QKt4	QKt—Q2
9	B—Kt2	Q—B2
10	Q—B2	P—K4

When the older players succeeded in playing this freeing advance, they used to throw their hats in the air and consider that the game was over. Nimzovich demonstrated in his theory of Pawn-chains, however, that the freeing advance is merely a natural prelude to a struggle in which both players have prospects.

11 O—O—O *!*

Eventual castling on the King-side is more natural, but in that event White is exposed to a strong attack after . . .

P—K5. On the Queen-side, however, the King is quite safe!

11 . . . .   P—K5

The alternative 11 . . . P × P; 12 P × P would be greatly in White's favor.

12 Kt—KR4 !

The reasoning behind this queer-looking move is this: a new Pawn-chain has been created with White's Pawn at K3 as the base. Black should attack this base with . . . P—B4—5 (when feasible); the Knight move is part of a maneuver which will make this advance impossible.

12 . . . .   Kt—Kt1
13 P—Kt3 !   Kt—K1

14 Kt—Kt2 !   P—B4
15 P—KR4 !

Completing the neutralizing maneuver: . . . P—B5 is unthinkable without the most elaborate preparations. This is indicative of the core of sound common sense imbedded in many of Nimzovich's weirdest-looking moves.

15 . . . .   B—Q1
16 P—R4

Resuming the Queen-side play, but first B—K2 and K—Q2 (as Nimzovich subsequently suggested) would have been more effective.

16 . . . .   P—QKt3 !

Instead of waiting to be throttled by encirclement strategy, Bernstein plays to open up the Queen-side for his own pieces.

17 P—Kt5   Kt—B3
18 Kt—B4   RP × P
19 RP × P   Q—B2
20 B—K2   B—B2
21 BP × P   B × Kt

After 21 . . . B × P; 22 Kt —R4 leaves Black with a very

difficult game. Therefore he
sacrifices a Pawn temporarily
in the hope of eventual freedom.

22 KtP × B	B—Q2
23 K—Q2	P × P
24 R—R1 !	

Thus we see the customary
result of an attack on the base
of a Pawn-chain: White has
opened up lines for maneuvering space.

24	Kt—B3
25 B × P	Kt—QR4
26 B—K2	KR—Kt1
27 Kt—R4 !	

The only chance of main-
taining the advantage; if 27 R
—QR3, R × P; 28 KR—R1,
Kt—B5 *ch;* 29 B × Kt, R × R;
30 B × P, Kt × B; 31 R × R,
P—R3 and White's winning
chances are meager. Nimzovich is angling for a Queen
sacrifice.

27	B × Kt
28 R × B	R × P

After 28 . . . Kt—B5 *ch;*
29 B × Kt, R × R; 30 Q × R,
P × B; 31 B—B3 the game
would take a very uncomfortable turn for Black, for example
31 . . . R × P; 32 Q—R8 *ch,*
Q—K1; 33 Q × Q *ch,* Kt × Q;
34 R—R1, R—Kt2; 35 R—
R5, P—Kt3; 36 P—Q5 *!* etc.

29 B—QB3 *!*	Kt—Kt6 *ch*

Giving White his chance;
but 29 . . . Kt—B5 *ch* leads
to the variation given above.

30 Q × Kt *!*	R × Q
31 R × R *ch*	Kt—K1

White has only Rook and
Bishop for the Queen, but his
strong invasion possibilities
promise a further gain of ma-
terial. However, the banal 32
KR—R1 *?* is met by 32 . . .
Q—B2 *!;* 33 R × Kt *ch,* K—
B2.

32 B—Q1 *!!*	R × B *!*

Rook retreats are no good: if 32 . . . R—Kt3 (or 32 . . . R—Kt8; 33 B—R4 !, R × R; 34 B × Kt ! and wins, while if 32 . . . R—Kt2; 33 B—R4, R—K2; 34 R—QKt1 followed by R(1)—Kt8 etc.); 33 B—R4, R—K3; 34 R—QKt1, Q—Kt3; 35 R(1)—Kt8, Q—Kt8; 36 B × Kt, Q × P *ch;* 37 K—B1 ! and wins!

33	K × R	Q—B2 *ch*
34	K—Q2	K—B2
35	B—R5 *ch!!*	P—Kt3

A fatal breach has been forced in Black's game.

| 36 | R(1)—R1 ! | Q—Kt3 |

After 36 . . . P × B; 37 R—R7 White wins easily.

37	B—K2	K—Kt2
38	K—K1 !	Kt—B2
39	R(8)—R5	K—R3
40	K—B1 !	

At Kt2 the King will be safe from attack and the first rank will be clear.

| 40 | . . . . | Q—Kt6 |
| 41 | P—R5 ! | Kt—K1 |

If 41 . . . Q—Kt7; 42 R(5)—R2 etc.

42	R—R6	Q—Kt7
43	P × P	P × P
44	R(6)—R2 !	Q—Kt2
45	R—R7	Q—Kt7

| 46 | K—Kt2 ! | |

Controlling the King Rook file and the seventh rank absolute, White threatens R—R1 mate! 46 . . . P—Kt4 is immediately refuted by 47 R(1)—R6 *ch*, while 46 . . . Q × B is answered by 47 R—R1 *ch*.

46	. . . .	Kt—B3
47	R—R1 *ch*	Kt—R4
48	B × Kt !	P × B
49	R(1)—R1 !!	Resigns

Black cannot contend with problem moves. This is one of Nimzovich's finest games.

26. Sophistication

YATES was famous for his brilliant play, and in this tournament he produced some of his very best chess. He was one of those players who live for the attack, and almost nothing else. (Most chess players follow their natural bent, and make no attempt to broaden their styles. It would have been just as impossible for Yates to play the subtly pointed, always refined, occasionally tortuous chess of Nimzovich, as it would have been for Nimzovich to play the always direct and occasionally naive chess of Yates.) How Nimzovich snatched the initiative from the great master of the attack makes an engrossing story.

RETI OPENING

Carlsbad, 1923
(First Brilliancy Prize)

WHITE: *F. D. Yates* BLACK: *A. Nimzovich*

1 Kt—KB3

Astonishing! Yates discards his beloved Ruy Lopez.

1	P—K3
2 P—KKt3	P—Q4
3 B—Kt2	P—QB3

Nimzovich is aiming at a Stonewall formation (to be completed by . . . P—KB4). It has the familiar drawbacks of weakening the black squares

and condemning the Queen's Bishop to inactivity.

4 P—Q3

It is clear that White does better with 4 P—Q4, with more possibilities of restraining Black. But Yates is apparently eager to play a King's Indian Defense with colors reversed.

4	B—Q3
5 Kt—B3	Kt—K2

[95

The King's Bishop's Pawn is to advance later on.

6 O—O   O—O
7 P—K4   P—QKt4 !

A daring conception, certainly one that few players would think of. Nimzovich wants play on the Queen-side, and is unmoved by such considerations as the weakening of his Pawn position or the enhanced power of White's fianchettoed Bishop.

8 Kt—K1   P—KB4
9 P × QP   KP × P
10 Kt—K2   Kt—Q2
11 B—B4

Yates plays to accentuate his opponent's weakness on the black squares by removing the

96]

protective Bishop. 11 P—QB4 was an excellent alternative.

11 . . . .   Kt—QKt3

Guarding the Bishop and preventing P—B4.

12 Q—Q2   Kt—Kt3
13 P—KR4

13 B × B, Q × B; 14 P—KB4, maintaining a firm grip on the black squares and keeping the enemy Knights out of play, looks more logical.

13 . . . .   Kt × B
14 Kt × Kt   Q—B3
15 P—QB3   B × Kt P

With this astonishing positional blunder, Nimzovich weakens his black squares and leaves himself with the inferior Bishop.

16 Q × B   Kt—R5
17 R—Kt1   Kt—B4
18 Q—K3   Q—Q3
19 P—KB4   B—R3

More likely to equalize is Nimzovich's suggestion 19 . . . Kt—Q2; 20 Kt—B3, Kt—B3; 21 Kt—K5, Kt—Kt5 etc.

20	Kt—B3	P—Kt5
21	KR—Q1	P × P
22	P × P	Kt—R5
23	Q—Q4	Q—R6

24 Kt—K5 *?!*

Correct was 24 R—Q2! Then if 24 . . . Kt × P; 25 R—Kt3, Q—B8 *ch;* 26 K—R2, Kt—Kt4; 27 Q—Kt4 threatening R—Kt1.

24	. . . .	Kt × P
25	R—K1	

Perhaps Yates had overlooked that 25 R—Kt3 *?* can be answered with 25 . . . Q × R!

25	. . . .	Kt × R
26	R × Kt	K—R1
27	P—R5	Q—Q3

28 K—B2 *?*

True to his style, Yates plays for attack. Correct was R—QB1—5, giving Black severe technical difficulties to surmount.

28	. . . .	QR—K1 *!*

He seeks counterplay.

29 P—R6 *?*

This attempt at attack gets him nowhere. R—QB1—5 was still better.

29	. . . .	Q × P
30	R—KR1	Q—B3
31	Q × RP	

31 . . . .   R × Kt *!!*

Sacrificing a whole Rook to begin a combination which re-

[97

deems the ragged play up to this point.

| 32 | P × R | Q × P |
| 33 | Q × B | Q—Q5 *ch* ! |

The first part of the combination, which is based on the lack of cooperation among White's forces. 33 . . . P—B5 ? is much weaker: 34 P × P, Q × P *ch*; 35 K—Kt1 or 34 . . . R × P *ch*; 35 B—B3.

34 K—B1

If instead 34 K—B3, P—B5 !; 35 R—K1 (if 35 P—Kt4 ? ?, Q—K6 mate, or 35 P × P ? ?, R × P *ch*; 36 K—Kt3, Q—B7 *ch* and mate next move), P × P *ch*; 36 K × P, Q —B7 *ch* and wins.

| 34 | . . . . | P—B5 |
| 35 | Q—R3 | |

Or 35 P × P, R × P *ch*; 36 K—K1 (36 K—K2 ? allows mate by 36 . . . R—B7 *ch* etc.), R—B1 !; 37 R—B1, R—K1 *ch* and wins. If 35 P—Kt4, P—B6; 36 B—R3, Q—K6; 37 R—R2, P—B7 wins.

| 35 | . . . . | K—Kt1 |
| 36 | R—R4 ! ♟ | P—Kt4 ! |

Not 36 . . . P × P *ch* ?; 37 Q × R *ch*!

| 37 | R—Kt4 | Q—R8 *ch* |
| 38 | K—B2 | |

More prosaic is 38 K—K2, R—K1 *ch*; 39 B—K4, P × B; 40 R × P *ch*, K—R1 and wins.

| 38 | . . . . | P × P *ch* |
| 39 | K × P | |

Or 39 K—K3, Q—Kt8 *ch* wins easily.

39	. . . .	Q—K4 *ch*
40	K—R3	P—R4
41	R—QR4	

If 41 R—Kt3, P—Kt5 *ch*; 42 K—R4, K—Kt2 ! and White is helpless against the double threat of . . . Q—B3 *ch* or . . . K—Kt3.

| 41 | . . . . | P—Kt5 *ch* |
| 42 | K—R4 | R—B4 ! |

Threatening 43 . . . Q—K8 mate or 43 . . . Q—R7 *ch* and mate next move.

43	R—R8 *ch*	K—Kt2
44	Q—R7 *ch*	K—R3
45	Q—Kt1	

Now the two mates are

guarded, but the position of White's Queen is a new misfortune:

45 . . . .   Q—B3 ch

White resigns, for if 46 K—

Kt3, R—B6 *ch!;* 47 B × R, Q × B *ch* and mate next move. The grand combination initiated with Nimzovich's 31st move was well worthy of a brilliancy prize!

27. Formula for Success

FEW players have possessed Nimzovich's gift for evolving powerful attacks from cramped positions. Everyone can admire the exultant, sweeping power of Black's concluding twelve moves in this game. But the real puzzle remains: "how did he arrive at that position?!"

The solution to the secret is this: *it was Nimzovich's system that gave him faith in apparently lifeless positions.* Reliance on the basic postulates enabled him to foresee, with uncanny prescience, the evolution of grand-scale attacks from puny beginnings. But such prevision requires faith, insight, self-confidence, patience; above all, it requires a thick hide, to resist the ridicule of the uncomprehending.

QUEEN'S INDIAN DEFENSE

Baden-Baden, 1925

WHITE: *E. Rabinovich*   BLACK: *A. Nimzovich*

1 P—Q4	Kt—KB3	
2 P—QB4	P—K3	
3 Kt—KB3	P—QKt3	
4 Kt—B3		

4 P—KKt3 is the move if White wants to play "scientifically" to maintain the initiative.

4	B—Kt2
5 B—Kt5	P—KR3
6 B—R4	B—K2
7 P—K3	P—Q3

The theoretical equalizing course is 7 . . . Kt—K5. This frees Black's game, but simplifies too much to suit the ambitious taste of a grand fighter like Nimzovich.

8 B—Q3	QKt—Q2
9 O—O	O—O
10 Q—K2	P—K4 ! ?

From a player with Nimzovich's crafty style, one would expect the slower and less direct 10 . . . Kt—R4. The text is the beginning of a daring strategical plan.

| 11 P × P | B × Kt ! |

First Black weakens his white squares by advancing his King's Pawn; then he weakens them still more by exchanging this Bishop. Why? The point is that 11 . . . P × P (or 11 . . . Kt × P; 12 Kt × Kt, P × Kt; 13 KR—Q1); 12 B—B5 ! would give White powerful pressure on the Queen's file. But only the further course of the game can fully explain Black's plan.

| 12 P × B |

Hoping for an attack via the King's Knight file—another problem for Black.

| 12 . . . . | Kt × P |
| 13 B × Kt ! ? |

A refined move. 13 B—B2 preserves the two Bishops with a promising game, but the text has its points: White removes the chief protection of his black squares, and relies on the drawing power of the Bishops on opposite colors if his game takes a turn for the worse.

13	B × B
14 B—K4	R—Kt1
15 QR—Q1	Kt—Q2 !

| 16 Kt—Q5 | Kt—B4 |
| 17 B—Kt1 | P—QR4 |

The Knight has greatly improved his position, and the text reinforces his hold on QB4.

18 K—R1	P—Kt3
19 R—Kt1	B—Kt2
20 R—Kt3	P—QB3 !

Having barricaded himself fairly well on the King's Knight file, Nimzovich begins to get the white squares under his control. His last move seems to weaken the Queen's Pawn critically, but there is method in his "madness."

| 21 Kt—B4 | R—Kt2 ! |
| 22 Q—B2 | Q—B3 ! |

23 P—Kt3

23 Kt—R5, Q × P; 24 R × KtP, P × R; 25 Q × P would be too wild for any hope of success.

The more moderate plan 23 Kt—R5, Q × P; 24 Kt × B, Q × Q; 25 B × Q, K × Kt; 26 R × P, R—Q2; 27 R × P would be defeated by 27 . . . R—Q7! The *decentralization* of White's forces can thus become a serious handicap.

| 23 . . . . | R—K1 |
| 24 Kt—K2 | |

He wants to centralize his Knight at Q4, incidentally closing the long diagonal. It would have been more consistent to play 24 QR—Kt1, keeping in reserve the idea of a sacrifice at Kt6.

| 24 . . . . | R—Q2 ! |

In order to answer 25 Kt—Q4 with 25 . . . P—Q4. Here at last we have the final explanation of Nimzovich's 11th move!!

| 25 R—Q2 | KR—Q1 |
| 26 Kt—B4 | |

Vacillation.

26 . . . .   K—B1

Edging away from danger.

27 Q—Q1   P—R4 *! !*

This masterly move will be the key to Black's final attack.

28 Q—Kt1   B—R3 *!*

Repulsing the attack: if 29 B × P, B × Kt or 29 Kt × P *ch*, P × Kt; 30 R × P, Q × P *ch*.

29 Kt—K2   P—Q4 *!*

At last!

30 P × P   R × P
31 R × R   R × R

Now the Queen file which White has spurned becomes a terrible weapon in Nimzovich's practiced hands.

32 P—B4

32 Kt—Q4 can be answered effectively by 32 . . . B—B5.

32 . . . .   B—Kt2 *!*

In order to keep the Queen file clear for future operations: thus 33 Kt—Q4 is answered by 33 . . . Q—Q3. Now that Nimzovich has the initiative, watch it grow!

33 Q—QB1

The sacrifice 33 B × P would have been refuted by the magnificent variation 33 . . . P—KR5 *!;* 34 R—Kt4, P × B; 35 R × KtP, Q—B4 *! !;* 36 R × B, Q—K5 *ch;* 37 Q—Kt2, R—Q8 *ch;* 38 Kt—Kt1, P—R6 *! !;* 39 Q × Q, Kt × Q with the fearsome threat of 40 . . . Kt × P mate! Watch that King's Rook Pawn!

33 . . . .   Q—Q3
34 B—B2   Kt—K5 *!*

The long-awaited exploitation of the Queen file winds up the game impressively.

35 R—Kt2   P—KR5 *!*
36 Kt—Kt1

If instead 36 P—KR3, Q—

Q2 *!*; 37 K—R2, R—Q7 and
wins.

36 . . . .   Kt—B6

37 P—R4

White reels from the hammer blows, but he fights on gamely. If 37 P—QR3, Kt—R7 wins the Queen's Rook Pawn.

37 . . . .   Kt—R7 *!*
38 Q—B1   Kt—Kt5 *!*
39 B—K4

Forced, but . . .

39 . . . .   R—Q8 *!*

40 Q—B4   P—KB4 *!*
41 B—B3   P—R6 *!*
42 R—Kt3   Kt—Q6 *!*

The mating threat appears again!

43 Q—B2   R—QB8
44 Q—K2   R—Kt8 *!*

White resigns, for if 45 R × RP, R—Kt7; 46 Q—B1, Kt × P *ch*; 47 K—Kt2, Kt × R *ch*; 48 K × Kt, P—KKt4 winning quickly. One of Nimzovich's most enjoyable games, and one of the finest in the whole range of chess literature!

28. "Nothing in Excess"

TO SAY that Nimzovich was the most original player who
ever lived, is no longer an impressive statement; the word
"original" has been used so often and so glibly that the word
has become pallid.

Let us put it this way: Nimzovich's moves were *more difficult to foresee* than those of any other player. The present
game probably illustrates this point more forcibly than any
other ever produced by Nimzovich.

Of course, originality is not merely a source of strength
and a potent weapon. It tires not only the opponent, but
oneself as well. And there always lurks the danger of degen-
erating into fussy, artificial over-elaboration.

NIMZOVICH ATTACK

Baden-Baden, 1925

WHITE: *A. Nimzovich*   BLACK: *S. Rosselli del Turco*

1	Kt—KB3	P—Q4
2	P—QKt3	P—QB4
3	P—K3	

A line of play with which
Nimzovich scored many successes. Often (as here) the
opening turned into a Nimzoindian Defense with colors
reversed.

3	. . . .	Kt—QB3
4	B—Kt2	B—Kt5
5	P—KR3	B × Kt

The retreat to R4 is more
elastic. If White then drives
the Bishop again with P—
KKt4, he weakens his Pawn
structure.

6	Q × B	P—K4

According to the classical
theory of the Pawn center,
Black has a powerful central
position. But Nimzovich now
proceeds to demonstrate that
the center Pawns are vulnera-

ble to hypermodern attack from the wings.

7 B—Kt5 !   Q—Q3

Nimzovich's basic strategy is to double Black's Queen Bishop Pawn. This could be accomplished at once, but Nimzovich defers the exchange until Black's Queen Pawn has been enticed to Q5, when Black's central Pawn mass will be immobile.

8 P—K4 !   P—Q5

Now White does not exchange, as Black can retake with the Queen.

9 Kt—R3 !   P—B3
10 Kt—B4   Q—Q2
11 Q—R5 *ch* !   P—Kt3

After 11 . . . Q—B2; 12 Q × Q *ch*, K × Q; 13 B × Kt, P × B the ending would be very unfavorable for Black because of his permanently weak Queen Bishop Pawns.

12 Q—B3   Q—QB2

See the note to Black's tenth move. If instead 12 . . . O—O—O; 13 Kt—R5 and Black cannot play 13 . . . KKt—K2 because of 14 Q × P.

13 Q—Kt4 !   K—B2

He still cannot castle. If 13 . . . Q—Q2 (not 13 . . . Kt —K2 ?; 14 Q—K6 and wins); 14 Q × Q *ch*, K × Q; 15 Kt— R5 forcing the doubling of the Pawn.

14 P—B4 ! !   P—KR4

Or 14 . . . P × P; 15 B × Kt !, P × B; 16 O—O, B—R3; 17 P—B3 !, R—Q1 (or 17 . . . P—Q6; 18 Q—B3, R—Q1; 19 Q—B2, Q—K2; 20 B—R3 and Black's position is completely disorganized); 18 B— R3 with powerful pressure.

15 Q—B3   P × P
16 B × Kt !   P × B

On 16 . . . Q × B Nimzo-
vich gives 17 Q × BP, R—K1;
18 O—O !, Q × P (if 18 . . .
R × P; 19 Kt—K5 ch and
wins); 19 Q—B7 ch !, Q—K2;
20 Kt—Q6 ch followed by 21
Kt × R and wins.

17 O—O   P—Kt4

Black is a Pawn ahead, but
his position is shattered. To
complete the demolition of his
game, Nimzovich needs three
Pawn moves: P—B3, P—K5
and P—KR4. They all appear
in due course.

18 P—B3 !   R—Q1

Capturing opens a mighty
diagonal for the White Bishop.

19 QR—K1 !   Kt—K2
20 P—K5 !   Kt—B4

If 20 . . . P—B4; 21 P—
KR4 ! smashes Black's Pawns.

21 BP × P !   Kt × P

Black has little choice, for if
21 . . . P × QP; 22 P × P, K
× P; 23 Q—K4 and Black is
helpless: 24 Q—K6 ch is
threatened. If 23 . . . Kt—
Kt6; 24 B × P ch wins; if 23
. . . Q—Q2; 24 Q—K5 ch.

22 Q—K4   B—K2

If 22 . . . P—B4; 23 Q—
Kt1, K—K3; 24 P—KR4 ! etc.

23 P—KR4 !   Q—Q2
24 KP × P   B × P
25 P × P   Resigns

If 25 . . . B—Kt2; 26 R ×
P ch, K—Kt1; 27 Q—Kt6 and
Black is left without a move.

29. Witches' Caldron

NIMZOVICH had a knack of conjuring complications out of even the simplest positions. He owed many a victory to his uncanny ability to infuse tension, uncertainty and ambiguity into positions which were inherently colorless.

In this game, for example, he meets his chief rival in the tournament. The lifeless opening play is of the kind that generally leads to a quick draw. But here both players are out for blood, and a thrilling struggle is the result.

INDIAN DEFENSE

Marienbad, 1925
(Special Prize)

WHITE: *A. Rubinstein*   BLACK: *A. Nimzovich*

1 P—Q4	Kt—KB3		5	P × P
2 Kt—KB3	P—QKt3		6 P—B4	P—Kt3
3 P—KKt3	P—B4		7 P—Kt3	B—Kt2
4 B—Kt2			8 B—Kt2	O—O
			9 O—O	

More exact is 4 P—Q5 and if 4 . . . B—Kt2; 5 P—B4.

4 . . . .   B—Kt2
5 P × P

After 5 O—O, P × P; 6 Kt × P, B × B; 7 K × B, Q—B1 the game generally takes on a drawish character. The text is objectively no better, but it leaves more scope for initiative.

If Nimzovich were interested in simplification, he could now play 9 . . . Kt—K5. But he naturally avoids this ignoble maneuver.

With both players in a fighting mood, it is important to perceive their strategical goals. White will aim at the occupation of Q5; Black will prepare strong counterplay on the Queen-side with . . . P—QR4–5.

9 . . . .   Kt—B3

The first surprise. Most players would continue 9 . . . P—Q3 and 10 . . . QKt—Q2, in order to leave the Queen Bishop an unimpeded diagonal and to play . . . Kt—Kt3 supporting the advance of the Queen Rook Pawn. However, Nimzovich prefers to proceed more obliquely—aside from which he hopes for an even more promising future for the Knight.

10 Kt—B3   P—QR4

Announcing that this Pawn will be ready to advance whenever White's Knight leaves QB3. Here and later, White

cannot very well advance his Queen Rook Pawn without seriously weakening his Queen Knight Pawn.

11 Q—Q2   P—Q3
12 Kt—K1

Rubinstein mistakenly thinks he has all the time in the world: he intends Kt—B2—K3—Q5. The proper course was 12 Kt—Q5 and if 12 . . . Kt × Kt; 13 B × B, K × B; 14 P × Kt, Kt—Kt5; 15 P—K4, P—R5 with a very interesting struggle in prospect. White would rely on his central Pawn mass, Black on his Queen-side counterplay.

12 . . . .   Q—Q2
13 Kt—B2   Kt—QKt5 !

If White turns peaceful now with 14 B × B, Q × B; 15 Kt × Kt, RP × Kt; 16 Kt—R4 Black can still preserve some initiative with 16 . . . Kt—Q2 followed eventually by . . . Kt—Kt3 to uncover the weakness of the Queen Rook Pawn.

14 Kt—K3   B × B
15 K × B

15 Kt × B was relatively better, despite the loss of time involved.

15 . . . .   Q—Kt2 *ch*

Obvious, but not easy to answer; for if 16 K—Kt1, Kt—K5; 17 Kt × Kt, Q × Kt and Black is set for . . . P—R5.

16 P—B3   B—R3 *!*

Just in time to forestall White's intended occupation of Q5. The pin has a very hampering effect on White's strategical. dispositions.

17 QKt—Q1

Apparently very strong: he guards the pinned Knight and threatens to ruin Black's Pawn position with 18 B × Kt.

How should Black counter the threat? One can see a "clever" draw arising from 17 . . . B—Kt2; 18 Kt—B3, B—R3; 19 QKt—Q1 etc.

17 . . . .   P—R5 *!*

He simply ignores the threat, for if 18 B × Kt, P × B; 19 Q × P, P × P and Black has a winning passed Pawn.

18 P × P

And now?!

18 . . . .   KR—K1 *! !*

One of the very finest moves ever played by Nimzovich. It establishes a kind of *Zugzwang* over the whole board, for if 19 P—QR3 (else simply 19 . . . R × P with powerful Queenside pressure), Kt—B3 to be followed by . . . R × P, not to mention such possibilities as . . . Kt—R4 or . . . Q—Kt6. The move seems to have a hypnotic effect on Rubinstein!

19 B × Kt   P × B
20 K—B2

Preparing for Q × P as well as P—B4. Is White safe?

20 . . . .   P—B4 *! !*

[109

White is a Pawn ahead and
is about to win a second Pawn,
yet his position is untenable.
If 21 P—B4 (else 21 . . . P—
B5; 22 P × P, B × P and the
permanent pin decides in
Black's favor), B—Kt2; 22
R—QKt1, B—Q5 !; 23 P—
QR3, Q—K5 with a winning
game.

21 Q × P   B—Kt2 !
22 R—QKt1   B—Q5

A magnificently centralized
Bishop. If now 23 R—Kt3 (not
23 P—QR3, Kt—Q6 ch), R—
K3; 24 Q—B4, Q—K2; 25 K
—Kt2 (else . . . Kt—B7), R
—K1 and White's position
caves in: 26 Kt—Q5, Kt × Kt;
27 P × Kt, R × P ch; 28 K—
R1, R × P threatening . . . Q
—K7.

110]

23 K—Kt2   B × Kt
24 Kt × B   R × Kt
25 Q × P

Rubinstein tries his luck
with pinning, but Nimzovich
slips out easily.

25 . . . .   R × P ch
26 R—B2   R × R ch
27 Q × R

Unfortunately he cannot re-
take with the King because of
27 . . . Kt—Q6 ch.

27 . . . .   R × P
28 P—QR3

Or 28 Q—Kt2, Q—B1 ! (the
most accurate) and the Knight
is unpinned.

28 . . . .   R × P
29 Q—K2   R—R1
30 P—B5   Q—R3
31 Q × Q   Kt × Q
32 R—QR1   Kt—B2
33 R × R ch   Kt × R

White resigned a few moves
later. Few players have had
Nimzovich's gift of making positional chess thrilling. It was
in recognition of this ability
that the game received a prize.

30. *Imitating the Inimitable*

IN ONE way, Nimzovich's inimitable maneuvering virtuosity had a pernicious effect on his impressionable disciples and imitators. His skill in handling difficult situations gave students a wholly inadequate conception of the drawbacks of a number of inferior opening variations. Hence some of Nimzovich's favorite lines have undergone radical revision, now that they can be appraised more objectively.

NIMZOINDIAN DEFENSE

Marienbad, 1925

WHITE: *K. Opocensky*

BLACK: *A. Nimzovich*

1 P—Q4	Kt—KB3
2 P—QB4	P—K3
3 Kt—QB3	B—Kt5
4 Q—B2	P—QKt3 ?

Very inferior, for with correct play on his opponent's part, Black will be left with a lifeless position. 4 . . . P—Q4 and 4 . . . P—B4 are the approved moves for disputing control of the center.

5 P—K4	B—Kt2
6 B—Q3	Kt—B3
7 Kt—B3	

White's first inexactitude, and of course not a fatal one:

7 Kt—K2 is more elastic, as it makes possible an early advance of the King Bishop Pawn with consequent domination of the center.

7 . . . .   B—K2 !

Since . . . B × Kt *ch* would only strengthen White's center, Nimzovich prefers to retain the Bishop. He gains time for retreating the Bishop because of the threat of . . . Kt—QKt5, which would remove White's valuable King Bishop.

8 P—QR3	P—Q3
9 O—O	P—K4
10 P—Q5	Kt—QKt1

[111

11 P—QKt4   QKt—Q2

Due to his inaccuracy on the seventh move, White has forfeited his chances of aggression via the King Bishop file. Nimzovich has therefore obtained a better game than he deserved!

White's proper positional plan is clearly indicated: to force P—B5. Therefore he should continue 12 P—KR3 to prepare for B—K3. Nimzovich suggests the plausible continuation 12 . . . P—KR3; 13 B —K3, P—KKt4; 14 Kt—KR2! and appraises White's Queenside attack as more promising than Black's counter on the opposite wing.

12 B—Kt2

The second inaccuracy: the

Bishop goes to the wrong diagonal. In the following play both adversaries have to combine action all over the board; Nimzovich succeeds admirably, Opocensky cannot quite keep step with him.

12 . . . .   O—O
13 Kt—K2   Kt—R4 *P!*

Instead of playing the indicated . . . Kt—K1 followed by . . . P—Kt3, Nimzovich deliberately provokes a Kingside attack, so as to deflect White's attention from the other wing!

14 Q—Q2

Note that White's last three moves have made the possibility of P—B5 more remote than ever. White could just as well have played 14 P—Kt4 at once, forcing the Knight back (if 14 . . . Kt—B5 *P*; 15 Kt × Kt, P × Kt; 16 P—K5 ! with strong initiative for White).

14 . . . .   P—Kt3
15 P—Kt4   Kt—Kt2
16 Kt—Kt3   P—QB3 !

Beginning the Queen-side counterplay.

17 Q—R6

Apparently very strong, but Nimzovich subtly demonstrates its hidden drawbacks.

17 . . . .   R—B1
18 QR—B1

If 18 K—R1 (intending 19 R—KKt1 and 20 Kt—B5), Black has an easy defense with 18 . . . P—B3, 19 . . . R—KB2 and 20 . . . B—B1.

18 . . . .   P—R3 !

From now on White must reckon with a possible smash-up of his Queen-side Pawns with . . . P—QKt4.

19 KR—Q1   R—B2
20 P—KR4 ?

Nimzovich's refutation of

this seemingly powerful move is characteristically ingenious.

20 . . . .   P × P !

White cannot very well re-take with the King Pawn, for then . . . P—QKt4 remains a formidable danger.

21 BP × P   R × R
22 R × R   Kt—B3

Forcing White's reply, for if 23 P—KKt5 ? ?, Kt—Kt5 wins the Queen! Or if 23 Kt—Kt5 ?, Q—Q2 !; 24 P—B3, R—B1 threatening . . . B—B1 ! with fatal effect.

23 Kt—R2   K—R1 !
24 Q—K3   Kt—Q2

To provoke 25 P—KKt5 ?, to which 25 . . . P—B3 ! is a very strong reply.

25 Kt—B3 !   Kt—B3

Not 25 . . . B × RP; 26 Kt × B, Q × Kt; 27 R—B7, B—B1; 28 B × RP with advantage to White.

26 Kt—R2   Kt—Kt1 !
27 P—KKt5

If 27 Kt—B3, B—B1 forces this move just the same.

[113

27 . . . .   P—B3 !

The King Bishop file is the road to victory.

28 Kt—B3   P × P
29 P × P   B—B1 !

Threatening 30 . . . B—Kt5 with deadly effect. The power of Black's forces is astounding, when one considers the slight amount of terrain at their disposal.

In the heat of the battle, Nimzovich does not overlook that the attractive 29 . . . R—B5 can be answered promisingly by 30 Kt × P !

30 R—B6 !

So that if 30 . . . B—Kt5; 31 Kt—R2, B × P; 32 Q × P. But Nimzovich forces the issue with:

30 . . . .   B—Q2 !
31 B × RP

The virtually forced sacrifice of the exchange (if 31 R × KtP ?, R × Kt) is very strong and must be met with the best play.

31 . . . .   B × R
32 P × B   Q—B2

33 P—Kt5

White is doing a good job of fishing in troubled waters: he hopes for 33 . . . Kt—K3; 34 P—R4, B—Q1; 35 B—R3, Q—B2 ?; 36 B × P !, Q × Kt; 37 B × P ch, Kt—Kt2; 38 Q × Q, R × Q; 39 P—B7 with advantage to White. But Nimzovich has a masterly reply.

33 . . . .   P—R3 ! !
34 P × P   Kt—K3
35 P—R4   B—Q1
36 B—R3   Q—B2 !

Now if 37 B × P ?, Q × Kt; 38 B × P ch, K—R2 winning easily! Or if 37 Kt—K1, B—Kt4 !; 38 Q × P, Kt—Q5; 39 Kt—Q3, B—K6 !; 40 P × B, Q—B6; 41 K—R2, Kt—K7 and wins.

37	Kt × P	P × Kt
38	B × R	Q × B
39	P—R5	Kt × P !
40	P × P	Kt—Kt5 !
41	P—B7	Kt × Q !
42	P—B8(Q)	Q—B6
43	P × Kt	Q × Kt ch

White resigns. The smartly calculated finish is a worthy conclusion to this great game. It was highly praised by Alekhine, who admired Nimzovich until the latter became a candidate for World Championship honors.

31. *Blunders and Brilliancies*

"TO ERR is human," we are told, and in this respect chess players are indeed human. Even the great masters are often afflicted with all too human frailty. Yet we would much rather have these grimly tense games than the sterile draws produced by chessic cookie-pushers. The mistakes of the masters give us a certain malicious pleasure, compensating for our own blunders; and (what is more important), these imperfect games generally take an attractively dramatic course. In their oversights, the grandmasters are like ourselves; in their great moments, they are inimitably and unapproachably themselves. Through it all the chess clock ticks for blunders as well as for brilliancies.

ALEKHINE'S DEFENSE

Semmering, 1926

WHITE: *A. Nimzovich*   BLACK: *Dr. A. Alekhine*

1	P—K4	Kt—KB3
2	Kt—QB3	P—Q4
3	P—K5	KKt—Q2

Nowadays 3 . . . P—Q5 is considered the safest reply, as the text can be answered by 4

[115

P—K6 *! ?*, P × P; 5 P—Q4.
White's sacrifice, quite in the
spirit of Nimzovich's theories,
justifies itself in a stifling blockade of Black's K4.

4	P—B4	P—K3
5	Kt—B3	P—QB4
6	P—KKt3	Kt—QB3
7	B—Kt2	B—K2
8	O—O	O—O

An interesting struggle is in
prospect. White has a "qualitative Pawn majority" on the
King-side, foreshadowing a
strong attack; Black stands
well in the center.

9	P—Q3	Kt—Kt3
10	Kt—K2	P—Q5

Intending to centralize a
Knight at Q4; but Nimzovich
criticizes the move, recom-
mending 10 . . . P—B3; 11
P × P, B × P followed by . . .
P—K4 with a good game.

11 P—KKt4 *! ?*   P—B3

But now this only weakens
Black's game. Nimzovich therefore suggests 11 . . . R—K1
(the "mysterious Rook move");
12 Kt—Kt3, B—B1 and P—
B5 is prevented.

116]

12	P × P	P × P
13	Kt—Kt3	Kt—Q4
14	Q—K2	B—Q3
15	Kt—R4	Kt(3)—K2

The possibility of 16 B × Kt
followed by 17 Kt—B5 is dis-
tasteful to Black.

16 B—Q2

Too slow. Nimzovich gives
16 Kt—R5 *!* with an aggressive position for White.

16	. . . .	Q—B2
17	Q—B2	

Again he misses the bus. Kt
—R5 was still more forceful.

17	. . . .	P—B5 *!*

This unforeseen diversion
gives Black strong counterplay.

| 18 P × P | Kt—K6 ! |
| 19 B × Kt | P × B |

Black must regain the sacrificed Pawn (if 20 Q × P??, B—B4 wins).

20 Q—B3	Q × P
21 Kt—K4	B—B2
22 P—Kt3	Q—Q5

And not 22 . . . Q × BP??; 23 QR—B1 winning a piece.

| 23 P—B3 | Q—Kt3 |
| 24 K—R1 | Kt—Q4 ? |

Already planning the maneuver . . . B—Q2—B3. But it would be better to use the Knight for defensive purposes and connect his Rooks with 24 . . . B—Q2.

25 P—B5 ?

Nimzovich's time is running short and he continues to flounder. He should have played (as he pointed out after the game) 25 P—Kt5 !, so that if 25 . . . P × P; 26 Kt × P, R × P?; 27 Q—R5 or 25 . . . P—B4; 26 Q—R5, P × Kt?; 27 B × P. If then 27 . . . R —B2; 28 P—Kt6 !, P × P; 29 Kt × P !, R—R2; 30 Kt—K7 ch !, R × Kt; 31 R—Kt1 ch followed by a quick mate.

25	Kt—B5 !
26 KR—Q1	K—R1
27 B—B1 !	P × P

A good move if Black follows it up properly . . . but he doesn't!

28 P × P	B—K4
29 R—K1	B—Q2
30 R × P	B—B3

The pin on the long diagonal looks menacing.

| 31 QR—K1 | Kt—Q4 ? |

Black is too absorbed in his plans. Either . . . QR—K1 ! or . . . R—KKt1 ! would have been far stronger.

| 32 R—Q3 | Kt × P ? |

And this proves fatal; he

should have played . . . Kt
—B5 followed by . . . QR—
K1 *!* or . . . R—KKt1 *!*

Black reckons only on 33 R
× Kt*?*, B × R; 34 Q × B, Q—
B7 *!* and wins.

33 Kt—Kt6 *ch !* P × Kt

He must take the Greek
gift: if 33 . . . K—Kt2; 34
Kt × R wins a piece, and if
33 . . . K—Kt1; 34 Kt—K7
ch ! with the same result.

34 Q—Kt4 *! !*

Much stronger than 34 P ×
P, K—Kt2; 35 Q—R3, R—R1;
36 R—Q7 *ch*, B × R; 37 Q ×
B *ch*, K × P and Black threatens 38 . . . R × P mate.

34 . . . .   R—B2 *?*

Nimzovich later demonstrated that there was a more tena-

cious defense with 34 . . . R
—KKt1; 35 P × P, K—Kt2; 36
R—Q7 *ch*, B × R; 37 Q × B
ch, K × P; 38 B—Q3 *!*, K—R3;
39 Q—R3 *ch*, K—Kt2; 40 R—
Kt1 *ch*, Q × R *ch !*

35 R—R3 *ch*   K—Kt2
36 B—B4 *! !*

Threatening mate in two,
and much stronger than 36 Q
× P *ch?*, K—B1; 37 R—R8
ch, K—K2; 38 R × R, Kt × Kt
and wins.

36 . . . .   B—Q4

Or 36 . . . P—Kt4; 37 Q
—R5 etc.

37 P × P *!*   Kt × Kt
38 P × R *ch*   K—B1
39 R × Kt

Even simpler was 39 Q—
Kt8 *ch*, K—K2; 40 P—B8(Q)
ch !, R × Q; 41 R—R7 *ch*, K
—K1; 42 Q × B etc.

39	B × R *ch*
40 Q × B	K—K2
41 P—B8(Q)*ch!*	R × Q
42 Q—Q5	Q—Q3
43 Q × P *ch*	K—Q1
44 R—Q3	B—Q5
45 Q—K4	R—K1
46 R × B	Resigns

An epic!

32. *The Manly Art*

OVER the centuries, chess devotees have allowed themselves to be maneuvered into a defensive position, subservient to all the popular prejudices that exist about the game. Yet it should be easy to make out a good case for chess. It is, as a rule, more tense than say boxing or football: athletic sports are full of physical action which relieves pent-up excitement, while chess offers no such outlet. The result is often an accumulated tension which explodes in a brilliant combination or, perhaps, a frightful blunder.

It is precisely for this reason that chess requires more *courage* than is needed for violent sports. For it is relatively easy to evoke the kind of fortitude that goes with strenuous physical exertion; the slow-burning, reflective courage which is needed in chess cannot be summoned up so readily. That is why all character defects reveal themselves so glaringly in chess play, and why they can be punished so relentlessly over the board.

DUTCH DEFENSE

Semmering, 1926
(Special Prize)

WHITE: *K. Gilg*   BLACK: *A. Nimzovich*

1 P—Q4	P—KB4	But this is far too timid.
2 P—KKt3	P—Q3	It deprives White's Queen Knight of his best square (QB3) and, worse yet, it betrays White's attitude of diffidence toward the great master.
A novel move.		
3 B—Kt2	Kt—KB3	
4 P—QB3 ?		He had better moves in 4

Kt—KB3 or P—QB4 or B—B4.

4 . . . .   Kt—B3
5 Kt—KR3

In view of Black's coming . . . P—K4, the Knight has little scope for action here.

5 . . . .   P—K4
6 O—O

6 B × Kt *ch*, P × B; 7 P × P, P × P; 8 Q × Q *ch*, K × Q would leave Black with a promising game despite the doubled, isolated Queen's Bishop Pawn.

6 . . . .   P—KR3 !

Preventing a possible Kt—Kt5 or B—Kt5 and preparing for an eventual mobilization of the King-side Pawn mass with . . . P—KKt4. We see that Black is as aggressive as his opponent is fearful.

7 P—B3

Repeating the pattern of his fourth move. But it is not easy to suggest something better.

In any event, his timidity will lead to more trouble.

120]

7 . . . .   P—Q4 *?!*

But this only leads to questionable complications. Consistent and strong was 7 . . . P—KKt4 !; 8 P—K4, P—B5 with a fine game for Black.

8 K—R1 ?

Still preparing—for what? The dynamic 8 P—K4 ! was clearly called for.

8 . . . .   B—Q3
9 P × P   Kt × P

Nimzovich has readily reconciled himself to loss of a Pawn, for after 10 P—KB4, Kt—B2; 11 B × P, Kt × B; 12 Q × Kt, O—O White would be behind in development and his weakness on the long diagonal would be worrisome.

10 Kt—Q2   O—O
11 P—K4

Even at this late date, the advance has a useful liberating effect on White's game.

11 . . . .   BP × P
12 P × P   Kt(4)—Kt5

If 12 . . . P × P; 13 Kt × P, Kt × Kt; 14 Q—Q5 *ch* etc. with altogether too much simplifying play for Nimzovich's taste. He therefore decides on an enterprising if inconclusive Pawn sacrifice.

13 R—K1   Q—K1 *! ?*
14 P × P   Q—R4

Threatening 15 . . . B × P *!*; 16 P × B *?*, Kt—B7 *ch* etc.

15 Kt—B1   B—QB4

Black has swung his Queen over to the King-side for aggressive action and he now threatens 16 . . . Q × Kt; 17 B × Q, Kt—B7 *ch* winning a piece. But 15 . . . B—Q2 (relying on faster development) may be preferable.

Luckily for Nimzovich, his opponent still continues to tremble over every move.

16 B—K3 *!*   B × B
17 Kt × B   B—Q2
18 Q—Q4 *!*

Finally preparing to mobilize his Queen's Rook. The apparently deadly 18 . . . Kt × Kt is to be met by 19 Kt—B4.

18 . . . .   QR—K1

Now the threat is 19 . . . Kt × Kt; 20 Kt—B4, Kt × B; 21 Kt × Q, Kt × R and wins.

19 Kt—B1 *?*

It was vital to remove one of the Knights: 19 Kt × Kt was correct.

19 . . . .   P—KKt4 *!*

Very important, in order to prevent Kt—B4.

20 Kt—Kt1 *?*

[121

The final milquetoast refusal to meet the issue: 20 K—Kt1 was in order.

| 21 Kt—R3 | Kt(Kt5)—B3 ! |
| 22 B × Kt | |

What else? If 22 Kt—B2, Kt × Kt *ch*; 23 Q × Kt, Kt—Kt5; 24 Q—Kt1, Kt—B7 *ch* winning the Queen; or 22 Kt—Kt1, Kt—B7 *ch !*; 23 Q × Kt, Kt—Kt5 with the same result.

22	Kt × B
23 Kt—Kt1	Kt—B7 *ch*
24 K—Kt2	B—R6 *ch*

| 20 . . . . | Kt—K5 ! |

Threatening a diversity of mates by . . . Kt—B7 *ch* or . . . Q × P *ch* or . . . Kt × P *ch*.

White resigns, for if 25 Kt × B, Q—B6 *ch*; 26 K—Kt1, Q—R8 mate (or 26 . . . Kt × Kt mate). A piquant game.

What this encounter teaches above all is that a player must consistently have the courage of his convictions.

33.   *A Miss is as Good as a Mile*

IN THE good old days before the first World War, Rubinstein was famous for his imperturbable precision. In those days he had the edge on his unruly colleague Nimzovich. After the war Rubinstein, his nerves shattered by his wartime experiences, was far more brilliant, but his oldtime steadiness had vanished. In the tournaments of the Twenties, he lost almost invariably to Nimzovich. In these games, one can sense Rubinstein's discomfort right in the opening stage: their "hypermodern" quality seems to irritate him, and he never recovers from this feeling throughout the game. The psychological odds are too great.

NIMZOVICH ATTACK

Semmering, 1926

WHITE: *A. Nimzovich*   BLACK: *A. Rubinstein*

1	Kt—KB3	P—Q4
2	P—QKt3	P—QB4
3	B—Kt2	Kt—QB3
4	P—K3	Kt—B3

It might be worth-while to play 4 . . . P—QR3, in order to prevent White's annoying reply, which enables him to play the Nimzoindian Defense with a move in hand. See also Game 37.

5	B—Kt5	B—Q2
6	O—O	P—K3
7	P—Q3	B—K2
8	QKt—Q2	O—O

Note the general similarity between the opening here and in Game 37.

9	KB × Kt	B × B

Both players are well satisfied with the exchange: Nimzovich because he gets control of K5, Rubinstein because he gets his beloved Bishop-pair.

10	Kt—K5	B—K1
11	P—KB4	Kt—Q2

Black is irked by the annoying presence of the advanced Knight and prepares to get rid of him in one way or another.

12	Kt × Kt	

Later Nimzovich recommended 12 Q—Kt4 as a stronger move. If then 12 . . .

Kt × Kt (12 . . . P—B3 is not feasible); 13 P × Kt with good attacking chances.

12	Q × Kt
13 P—K4	P—B3

To give his Queen's Bishop more scope.

14 Q—B3	B—B2
15 P—QR4	P—QKt3

Black is probably better off with 15 . . . P—Q5, blocking the hostile Bishop's diagonal and keeping the King file closed.

16 QR—K1	P—QR3

. . . P—Q5 was still possible.

17 P—B5	QP × P

Giving White a powerful post at K4 for his pieces. Black had better moves in 17 . . . P—Q5 or . . . P—K4 or . . . KR—K1. Note, however, that 17 . . . KP × P is answered by 18 P × QP *!*, for if 18 . . . B × P *?;* 19 R × B *!*

18 Q × P *!*	P—K4
19 R—K3	P—QKt4
20 R—Kt3	

Planning a King-side attack (the threat is 21 Q—KKt4 winning a piece, for if 21 . . . P —Kt3; 22 P × P, Q × Q; 23 P × B *ch*).

20	K—R1
21 Kt—B3	P × P *?*

Careless: he should have played 21 . . . B—Q3.

22 Kt × P *! !*	Q—K1

And not 22 . . . P × Kt; 23 Q × KP, B—B3; 24 Q × B *!*, P × Q; 25 B × P mate! This is the first of many instances in which White's Bishop plays an important role (see the earlier notes in which . . . P—Q5 was recommended!).

23 Q—KKt4	KR—Kt1

24 Kt × B *ch*

A pardonable slip in over-the-board play. The bottled-up state of Black's King allows the following fine win subsequently discovered by Kurt Emmerich: 24 Kt—Kt6 *ch !*, B × Kt; 25 P × B, P—R3 (inevitable); 26 R—R3, Q—KB1 (if 26 . . . P × P; 27 Q—Kt5 *! !*, Q—KB1; 28 R × P *!*, B × R; 29 B × B followed by 30 R × P *ch* and mate next move); 27 Q—Kt5 *!*, P—R6 *!*; 28 B—R1, R—Q1 *!*; 29 R × P *!*, R—Q5 *!*; 30 R × P *ch !*, P × R; 31 R—B7 *! !* (more conclusive than 31 P—Kt7 *ch*), R—Kt2 (if 31 . . . Q × R; 32 Q × P *ch* or if 31 . . . Q—Kt2; 32 R × Q, R × R; 33 Q—B5 *!*, P—QR4; 34 Q—QB8 *ch*, R—Kt1; 35 Q—Q7, R—Kt2; 36 Q—K8 *ch* and wins); 32 R × Q *ch*, B × R; 33 Q—B5 *!*, R—Q1; 34 Q—B7, P—QR4; 35 P—KKt4 followed by P—R4 and wins.

24	Q × Kt
25 Q × P	Q—Q4
26 Q—KKt4	B—Q1
27 Q—Kt6 *!*	

Not only is the Queen im-

mune from capture, but White is even threatening 28 Q × RP *ch !* and mate next move!

27	P—R3
28 R—K1	Q—Q2
29 R—K6	

29 R—K4 was simpler; the text is the beginning of a combination which White has to renounce on the following move because of time pressure.

| 29 . . . . | P—B5 *P !* |

30 KtP × P

Harried by the clock, Nimzovich recoils from the decisive but winning combination 30 R × BP *!*, B × R; 31 B × B, P × B; 32 Q × RP *ch*, Q—R2; 33 Q × P *ch*, R—Kt2; 34 R—Kt6 *!*, K—Kt1; 35 R—R6,

R—KB2; 36 Q—Kt5 ch, R—
Kt2; 37 Q—R5 ! and Black's
Queen is lost.

30	R—Kt1
31 B—B3	R—Kt8 ch
32 R—K1	B—Kt3 ch ?

Not the best; after 32 . . .
R × R ch; 33 B × R, Q—R5 !
White would still have serious
technical difficulties.

33 K—B1	R × R ch
34 B × R	Q—R5
35 R—R3 !	R—KB1

Other Rook moves permit
the sacrifice of White's Rook,
for instance 35 . . . R—K1; 36
R × P ch !, P × R; 37 Q ×
RP ch, K—Kt1; 38 Q—Kt6 ch,
K—R1; 39 Q × P ch, K—Kt1;
40 B—B3 ! (see the note to
Black's 32nd move).

| 36 B—B3 | B—Q1 |

A longer but hopeless resist-
ance could be made with 36
. . . Q × P(7); 37 R × P ch,
P × R; 38 Q × RP ch, K—
Kt1; 39 Q—Kt6 ch, K—R1;
40 B × P ch, R × B; 41 Q ×
R ch, K—Kt1; 42 Q × B, Q ×
QP ch etc. The text, on the

other hand, allows a drastic
finish.

37 B—Q2	Q × P(7)
38 B × P	Q—Kt8 ch
39 K—K2	Q—B7 ch
40 K—K3 ! !	

Stronger than the more obvious 40 B—Q2 ch.

| 40 . . . . | B—Kt3 ch |

On 40 . . . Q—B8 ch Nim-
zovich planned this piquant
win: 41 K—K4 !, Q—K8 ch;
42 R—K3 !, Q—R5 ch; 43 K
—Q5 !, P × B; 44 R—R3 and
wins.

| 41 K—K4 ! | Q—K7 ch |
| 42 R—K3 ! | Resigns |

An engrossing game.

34. Improvisation Fails

ARE the opponents in this game Yates and Nimzovich, or Yates and "the system"?! One wonders. For what we see here is the unequal struggle between naive traps and spasmodic attacking attempts and the steadily accumulating force of quiet moves played according to a general theory. Improvisation cannot make up for the absence of a middle game compass.

FRENCH DEFENSE

Semmering, 1926

WHITE: *F. D. Yates*   BLACK: *A. Nimzovich*

1 P—K4	P—K3		*7*	B—Kt5
2 P—Q4	P—Q4			
3 Kt—QB3	B—Kt5			
4 P × P				

Too tame: 4 P—K5 is the only chance for initiative.

4 . . . .   P × P
5 B—Q3   Kt—K2

This development (more elastic than . . . Kt—KB3) was a great favorite with Nimzovich.

6 Kt—K2   O—O
7 O—O

7 Kt—Kt3 looks more promising.

7 . . . .   B—Kt5

The pin is irritating for White, who lacks maneuvering space. He is provoked to create a weakness by:

8 P—B3   B—KR4
9 Kt—B4   B—Kt3
10 QKt—K2   B—Q3
11 Q—K1 ?

Apparently playing for "attack." Nimzovich rightly recommends 11 B × B, RP × B; 12 Kt—Q3, guarding the squares K5 and QB5. The latter point is particularly vital, for Black can exploit the weakness on his K6 only by . . . P

[127

—QB4 in combination with
. . . R—K1.

11	P—QB4 *!*
12 P × P	B × P *ch*
13 K—R1	QKt—B3
14 B—Q2	R—K1

Black has his guns trained
on K6.

15 Kt × B	RP × Kt
16 P—KB4 *?*	

Still seeking the attack. The
esults are grievous.

16	Kt—B4

With three pieces bearing
down on the weak point,
Black's positional advantage is
clear.

17 P—B3	P—Q5 *!*

White's last move was necessary to keep Black's Knights
out of Q4, but the text forces
the issue.

18 P—B4	Q—Kt3 *!*

A many-sided move: he prevents counterplay by P—
QKt4; he strengthens the pressure on K6; and he prepares to
remove White's King Bishop,
which blockades the passed
Pawn.

19 R—B3	

So that if 19 . . . Q × P *?*;
20 R—Kt1, Q × P (if 20 . . .
Q—R6; 21 B × Kt); 21 R—
R1 with at least a draw. But
Nimzovich has a far stronger
retort.

19	B—Kt5 *!*

Removing the most impor-
tant protection of White's K3
and thus preparing for the occupation of that point.

20 P—QR3	B × B
21 Q × B	P—R4 *!*
22 Kt—Kt1	R—K6
23 R—Q1	QR—K1
24 Q—KB2	Q—Kt6 *!*

Black has made appreciable
progress: he has a strongly
centralized outpost in the only

open file, and he now proceeds to lift the blockade of his passed Pawn.

25 R—Q2	Kt—Q3 !
26 P—QB5	Kt—B5
27 B × Kt	Q × B

Nimzovich has smashed the blockade, and White's Pawn position is weaker than ever.

| 28 R—B2 | Q—Q4 |
| 29 R—B1 | Q—K5 |

Intensifying the centralized control of the open file. The threat of 30 ... R × R; 31 Q × R, Q × Q; 32 Kt × Q, R—K7 forces action on White's part.

30 P—B5 ! ?	R × R
31 Kt × R	Q × P
32 P—QKt4	

The point; but Nimzovich sees further ahead.

32	P × P
33 P × P	Kt × P
34 Q × P	Kt—Q6 !

Forcing White's reply, for if 35 R—B3 (or 35 R—B4), R—K8 *ch !*; 36 Kt × R, Q—B8 *ch*; 37 Q—Kt1, Kt—B7 mate.

35 R—B2

| 35 .... | R—QB1 ! |

Avoiding the diabolical trap 35 ... Kt—K8 ?; 36 R—K2 *! !*, R × R; 37 Q—Q8 *ch*, K—R2; 38 Kt—Kt5 *ch*, K—R3; 39 Kt × P *ch*, K—R4; 40 Q—R8 *ch*, K—Kt5; 41 Q—R3 ch, K—B5; 42 Q—Kt3 *ch*, K—K5; 43 Kt—Q6 *ch* winning the Queen! (Nimzovich).

| 36 R—B3 | Kt × P |

[129

Although two Pawns ahead, Black is now forced on the defensive. However, continual offers of exchanges set off his advantage.

37 P—R4	P—Kt3
38 Kt—Kt5	R—B1
39 R—B3	Q—Q2
40 Q—QB4	Kt—K3
41 R—Q3	Q—B1

For if 42 Q × Q, R × Q; 43

Kt × Kt, P × Kt; 44 R—Q6, R—Kt1 and wins.

42 Q—Kt5	Q—B8 *ch*
43 K—R2	Q—B5 *ch*
44 P—Kt3	Q—B7 *ch*
45 K—R1	Q—B8 *ch*
46 K—R2	Kt—B4

White resigns, for if 47 R—Kt3, Q—B7 *ch* etc. Position play of a high order!

35.   *Hard to Beat*

FOR profundity, precision and originality this game is hard to beat even in the distinguished roster of great Nimzovich games. The game did even more, perhaps, than his first prize in the tournament to convince the chess world of his greatness. Such a noted judge of great chess as Irving Chernev rates this game among his special favorites. Logic and originality are inextricably fused here.

NIMZOINDIAN DEFENSE

Dresden, 1926
(First Brilliancy Prize)

WHITE: *P. Johner*   BLACK: *A. Nimzovich*

1 P—Q4	Kt—KB3
2 P—QB4	P—K3
3 Kt—QB3	B—Kt5

| 4 P—K3 | O—O |

Nimzovich has adopted what is probably the best reply

to Rubinstein's innocent-look-
ing 4 P—K3. Castling leaves
Black his freedom of choice
among many possibilities.

5 B—Q3   P—B4

This would also have been a
good reply to 5 Kt—K2.

6 Kt—B3   Kt—B3
7 O—O   B × Kt
8 P × B   P—Q3

Nimzovich is confronted
with the problem which this
opening so frequently offers:
how can Black exploit the doubled Pawn?

9 Kt—Q2 !   P—QKt3

On 9 . . . P—K4 White has
a satisfactory reply in 10 P—
Q5, Kt—QR4; 11 Kt—Kt3.

10 Kt—Kt3 ?

But this is a mistake, says
Nimzovich, and he recom-
mends 10 P—B4, P—K4; 11
BP × P, QP × P; 12 P—Q5,
Kt—QR4; 13 Kt—Kt3, Kt—
Kt2; 14 P—K4, Kt—K1. In
that event White would have
the open King Bishop file,
while the square K2 would be
available for his Queen.

10 . . . .   P—K4

See the result of White's
poor timing: if 11 P—Q5, P—
K5 ! with a fine game.

11 P—B4   P—K5
12 B—K2

At B2 the Bishop has even
less of a future.

12 . . . .   Q—Q2 ! !

Black's task (which he carries out impeccably) is to restrain or neutralize the pros-
pective advance of White's
King-side Pawns. The text is a
shocking violation of orthodox
rules, as Black's Queen blocks
his Bishop.

13 P—KR3   Kt—K2
14 Q—K1

White has nothing better: if 14 B—Q2 (or 14 P—Kt4, P—Kt3 and White can make no further progress), Kt—B4; 15 Q—K1, P—Kt3; 16 P—Kt4, Kt—Kt2 and again White's Pawns are rendered innocuous.

14 . . . .   P—KR4 !

Now the blockading process is in full swing.

15 B—Q2

With 15 Q—R4, Kt—B4; 16 Q—Kt5 White would only be heading for trouble: 16 . . . Kt—R2; 17 Q × P, Kt—Kt6 winning the exchange.

15 . . . .   Q—B4 !
16 K—R2   Q—R2 ! !

Nimzovich has completed

the hemming-in of White's qualitative Pawn majority. The next step, which requires the utmost mastery, is to provoke the stabilization of the center with P—Q5.

17 P—QR4   Kt—B4

Innocent as the move looks, it threatens 18 . . . Kt—Kt5 *ch;* 19 P × Kt, P × P *ch;* 20 K—Kt1, P—Kt6 and wins.

18 P—Kt3   P—R4 !

Nimzovich takes the risk of making his Queen Knight Pawn backward in order to stifle White's counterplay by P—R5 etc.

19 KR—Kt1 !   Kt—R3
20 B—KB1

White clears the second rank for defensive action.

20 . . . .   B—Q2
21 B—B1   QR—B1
22 P—Q5

White can take a hint; he advances the Pawn before . . . B—K3 initiates uncomfortable pressure. But now the center is closed, and Black is ready to

attack on the King-side without fear of diversion.

22 . . . .   K—R1 *!*
23 Kt—Q2   KR—Kt1

Now the King Knight file is
to be opened, and the strategic significance of Black's
Queen maneuver takes on tactical overtones.

24 B—KKt2

Setting up a microscopic
hope of counterplay against
the hostile King Pawn.

24 . . . .   P—KKt4 *!*
25 Kt—B1   R—Kt2
26 R—R2   Kt—B4
27 B—R1   QR—KKt1

Black's position has reached
the state of maximum power,
and the decisive stage has been
reached. The attack will have
to be managed very resource-
fully, as White is stripped for
action on the second rank and
has his eye on the King's Pawn.

28 Q—Q1   P × P

Opening the attacking file,
but also jeopardizing the
King's Pawn.

29 KP × P   B—B1 *!*
30 Q—Kt3   B—R3

31 R—K2

Counterplay. Against the
passive defensive maneuver B
—Q2—K1 Nimzovich had
planned a beautiful combination: 31 B—Q2, R—Kt3 *!;* 32
B—K1, Kt—Kt5 *ch !;* 33 P ×
Kt (if 33 K—Kt2, B × P *!*
wins), P × P *ch;* 34 K—Kt2,
B × P *!;* 35 Q × B, P—K6 *!*
and White can stop mate only
by losing his Queen after 36
Kt × P, Kt × Kt *ch*. A wonderfully imaginative conception!

31 . . . .   Kt—R5
32 R—K3

Nimzovich tells us that he

[133

had expected 32 Kt—Q2, which he intended to answer with 32 . . . B—B1 *!;* 33 Kt × P (if 33 Q—Q1, B × P *!;* 34 K × B, Q—B4 *ch* and wins), Q—B4; 34 Kt—B2, Q × P *ch !;* 35 Kt × Q, Kt—Kt5 mate!

| 32 . . . . | B—B1 *!* |
| 33 Q—B2 | B × P *!* |

For if 34 K × B, Q—B4 *ch;* 35 K—R2, Kt—Kt5 *ch;* 36 K —R3, Kt—B7 *ch;* 37 K—R2, Q—R6 mate.

| *34* B × P | B—B4 |

The Bishop retires discreetly, making room for the murderous advance . . . P—R5.

| *35* B × B | Kt × B |
| *36* R—K2 | P—R5 |

Now White's position crumbles.

37 R(1)—Kt2	P × P *ch*
38 K—Kt1	Q—R6
39 Kt—K3	Kt—R5
40 K—B1	R—K1 *!*

White resigns. Nimzovich points out that if 41 K—K1 (the threat was 41 . . . Kt × R; 42 R × Kt, Q—R8 *ch;* 43 K— K2, Q × R *ch* etc.), Kt— B6 *ch;* 42 K moves, Q—R8 *ch* leading to mate.

A great game. It lifts originality to monumental heights.

36.   *Stresses and Strains*

FEW masters have been as keenly sensitive as was Nimzovich to all the subtle details of a given Pawn formation. It was this unique quality which enabled him to make startling moves, involving apparent Pawn weaknesses. With his unrivalled understanding of the stresses and strains to which Pawn positions are subjected, he knew just how far he could go in taking liberties with orthodox conceptions.

These surprise moves often had great psychological value. In this game, for example, so great a master as Rubinstein is bewildered right in the opening: he chooses bad moves, deprives himself of the best defensive resources. Of course, the later play has many of the piquant details for which Nimzovich is so famous. They exhaust the exclamation mark!

ENGLISH OPENING

Dresden, 1926

(Prize for the best-played game)

WHITE: *A. Nimzovich*   BLACK: *A. Rubinstein*

1 P—QB4	P—QB4
2 Kt—KB3	Kt—KB3
3 Kt—B3	P—Q4
4 P × P	Kt × P
5 P—K4 *! ?*	

The usual move is 5 P—KKt3, but for Nimzovich the usual was unusual.

5 . . . .   Kt—Kt5

Beginning an adventure which turns out badly. Simple and satisfactory was 5 . . . Kt × Kt; 6 KtP × Kt, P—KKt3; 7 P—Q4, B—Kt2 transposing into an excellent variation of the Gruenfeld Defense.

6 B—B4 *!*

The astute authority on Pawn formations is not particularly worried about the hole at Q3.

6 . . . .   P—K3

Against Takacs at Rogaska-Slatina, 1929, Rubinstein tried 6 . . . Kt—Q6 *ch* and there followed 7 K—K2, Kt × B *ch* (if 7 . . . Kt—B5 *ch;* 8 K—B1 threatening P—Q4); 8 R × Kt, P—QR3; 9 P—Q4 *!,* P × P; 10 Q × P, Q × Q; 11 Kt × Q, P—K3; 12 Kt—R4 *! !,* Kt—Q2; 13 KR—Q1, P—QKt4; 14 Kt × KP *! !,* BP × Kt; 15

B × KP, P × Kt; 16 R × B *ch !* and wins.

7 O—O   QKt—B3

Leaving the other Knight in an awkward situation. However, if he reserves QB3 for the retreat of the advanced Knight, then the development of his Queen-side becomes a problem.

8 P—Q3   Kt—Q5

Something has to be done about the threatened P—QR3.

9 Kt × Kt   P × Kt
10 Kt—K2

What a change from the previous diagram! The attack on White's Q3 is covered up; Black has a weak Queen's Pawn (. . . P—K4 opens a strong diagonal for White); White's mobile Pawn formation on the King-side gives him good attacking chances.

10 . . . .   P—QR3

Further postponement of orderly development; but if 10 . . . B—K2; 11 B—Kt5 *ch* and interposition costs a Pawn: 11 . . . B—Q2; 12 Kt × P or 11

. . . Kt—B3; 12 Q—R4, B—Q2; 13 B × Kt, B × B; 14 Q × QP etc.

11 Kt—Kt3   B—Q3
12 P—B4

Stronger, says Nimzovich, was 12 Q—Kt4. Then if 12 . . . O—O (a trifle better is 12 . . . Q—B3; 13 P—B4 with a very strong game for White); 13 B—KKt5 *!*, B—K2 (if 13 . . . P—K4; 14 Q—R4 with a view to Kt—R5 and Kt × P); 14 B—R6, B—B3; 15 B × KtP, B × B; 16 Kt—R5 and wins.

12 . . . .   O—O
13 Q—B3

He has powerful alternatives in 13 P—K5 or P—B5.

13 . . . .   K—R1
14 B—Q2   P—B4

Partly to prevent the formidable P—B5, partly to provoke P—K5 blocking the King file. But the Queen's Pawn will be weaker than ever.

15 QR—K1

Nimzovich writes that he owns preferred stock in the

King file! And it is an invest-
ment that will yield very hand-
some dividends.

15 . . . .   Kt—B3
16 R—K2   Q—B2

A slight inexactitude which
bulks large later on. Correct
was the more elastic . . . B—
Q2, reserving the possibility of
a later . . . Q—B3. As Rubinstein plays, his Queen is cut off
from the defense of the King-
side.

17 P × P   P × P

18 Kt—R1 ! !

White's King Bishop has a
powerful diagonal. Nimzovich
intends Kt—B2—R3—Kt5 fol-
lowed by Q—R5, which will
force further weaknesses.

18 . . . .   B—Q2
19 Kt—B2   QR—K1
20 KR—K1   R × R
21 R × R   Kt—Q1

The intended 21 . . . R—K1
is met by 22 Q—Q5 !, Kt—K2;
23 Q—B7 and Black suffo-
cates.

22 Kt—R3   B—B3

The Queen must be brought
to the defense: if 22 . . . R—
K1; 23 Q—R5, R × R; 24 Kt
—Kt5, P—R3; 25 Q—Kt6,
P × Kt; 26 Q—R5 mate.

23 Q—R5   P—KKt3

Unavoidable, but now the
maneuver begun with 18 Kt—
R1 ! ! has achieved its purpose.
The weakness on the long diagonal will prove fatal.

24 Q—R4   K—Kt2
25 Q—B2 ! !

Forcing Black to deflect his
Queen or King's Bishop from
the defense.

25 . . . .   B—B4

25 . . . Q—Kt3 allows 26
P—QKt4 ! followed by 27 B—
B3 !

[137

26 P—QKt4 *!*   B—Kt3

Exile from the King-side.

27 Q—R4 *!*   R—K1

The solid-looking 27 . . . R
—B3 leads to immediate col-
lapse: 28 Kt—Kt5, P—R3; 29
Kt—R7!

28 R—K5 *!!*

28 . . . .   Kt—B2

What to do about the out-
post in the open file? If 28
. . . R × R; 29 P × R winning
easily (29 . . . Q × P; 30 Q—
R6 *ch* and mate next move).
If 28 . . . P—R3; 29 P—Kt4 *!*,
P × P (if 29 . . . P—Kt4; 30
BP × P *!*); 30 P—B5 *!*, Q ×
R; 31 P—B6 *ch !*, Q × P; 32
Q × P mate (Nimzovich).

29 B × Kt *!*   Q × B

Or 29 . . . R × R; 30 P × R,
Q × B; 31 Kt—Kt5, Q—Kt1;
32 P—K6 followed by Q—B4
winning.

30 Kt—Kt5   Q—Kt1
31 R × R   B × R
32 Q—K1 *!!!*   B—B3

Because of the banishment
of his King's Bishop, Black is
helpless against an invasion on
his K4 or K2. Thus:
   I   32 . . . P—R3; 33 Q—
K5 *ch*, K—B1; 34 Q—B6 *ch*,
B—B2; 35 P—Kt5 *!*, B—B4;
36 Kt—K6 *ch*, K—K1; 37 Q—
Q8 mate.
   II   32 . . . K—B1; 33 Q—
K5, B—Q1 (if 33 . . . Q × P;
34 Q—B6 *ch*, K—Kt1; 35 Kt
—K6); 34 Kt—K6 *ch*, K—K2;
35 Q—B5 *ch !*, K—Q2; 36 Kt
—B8 *ch !* and wins.

33 Q—K7 *ch*   K—R1

If 33 . . . K—R3; 34 Kt—
K6 decides.

34 P—Kt5 *!*

A nice touch. If now 34 . . .
P × P; 35 Kt—K6, P—R4; 36
Q—B6 *ch*, K—R2; 37 Kt—

Kt5 *ch*, K—R3; 38 B—Kt4 *!*
followed by mate. Hence Rubinstein despairingly gives up
a piece. Resignation would
have been more graceful.

34	Q—Kt2
35 Q × Q *ch*	K × Q
36 P × B	P × P
37 Kt—B3	P—B4
38 Kt—K5	B—B2

39 Kt—B4	K—B2
40 P—Kt3	B—Q1
41 B—R5	B—K2
42 B—B7	K—K3
43 Kt—Kt6	P—R3
44 P—KR4	P—Kt4
45 P—R5	P—Kt5
46 B—K5	Resigns

Nimzovich was justifiably
proud of this enchanting game.

37. Change is Permanent

TIMES change, and with them men and their ways of
thinking. In chess, the changes are in the direction of ever
greater refinement. In nineteenth-century chess, sacrifices
of material were popular and highly prized. In modern
chess, we see a "higher" type of combination, which is not
so easy to appreciate. This is the sacrifice of position, less
tangible but just as real as the old-time fireworks. When, for
example, Nimzovich "sacrifices" control of the Queen file to
a great master like Vidmar, he is taking as great a risk as
ever Morphy and Anderssen took in sacrificing material in
the grand manner.

What a pity it is that from the point of view of gaining
appreciation, this modern form of sacrifice is so subtle that
it passes almost unnoticed! What painful irony there is in
the fact that those very aspects in which the master dis-
plays his greatness are the ones that are most deeply
concealed from the public! The resulting time lag has

often made for tragic consequences; for the master feels misunderstood, while the public is mystified.

QUEEN'S INDIAN DEFENSE

New York, 1927

WHITE: *Dr. M. Vidmar*　　　　　BLACK: *A. Nimzovich*

1	P—Q4	Kt—KB3
2	Kt—KB3	P—K3
3	P—B4	B—Kt5 *ch*
4	B—Q2	Q—K2

A characteristic Nimzovich waiting move which offers more possibilities than the immediate . . . B × B *ch*.

5 Kt—B3

5 P—KKt3 is the move which holds out the greatest prospects of yielding an advantage for White.

5	. . . .	O—O

5 . . . P—QKt3, leading directly to the text continuation, was more accurate.

6 P—K3

. . . For White could have played 6 Q—B2, P—Q3 (Black must take measures

against the coming advance of the King's Pawn); 7 P—K4, P—K4; 8 P—Q5 and White is better off than in the game.

6	. . . .	P—Q3
7	B—K2	

The apparently more aggressive B—Q3 is effectively answered by . . . P—K4.

7	. . . .	P—QKt3
8	O—O	B—Kt2
9	Q—B2	QKt—Q2

10 QR—Q1

Vidmar is playing too many dull, "simple" moves. Better was 10 Kt—KKt5 and if 10 . . . P—KR3; 11 B—B3 *!* greatly improving his position.

The text is a warning to Black to avoid the opening of the Queen file; but Nimzovich is not intimidated.

10 . . . .   B × Kt

"Eventually, why not now?"

11 B × B   Kt—K5
12 B—K1   P—KB4

The logic of the situation is quite clear: Black plays for control of K5 plus attacking chances; White wants exchanges and line-opening, so that his Bishops can be useful.

13 Q—Kt3   P—B4 *! ?*

Indicating that he does not fear the opening of the Queen file later on.

14 Kt—Q2   Kt × Kt
15 R × Kt   P—K4 *!*
16 P × KP

Vidmar is true to his plan: 16 P—Q5 blocks the hostile

Bishop's diagonal, to be sure, but it penalizes White's Rooks similarly, and Black can still work up a good attack by . . . P—B5 or . . . P—K5.

16 . . . .   P × P
17 P—B3   P—KKt4 *!*

Nimzovich shuns no risk! In the days of Tarrasch, Black would have played his Rooks to the Queen file, ending up in a lifeless draw.

18 B—B2   Kt—B3
19 KR—Q1   QR—K1 *!*
20 Q—R4   B—R1 *!*

Guarding against the double threat of 21 R—Q7 and 21 Q × P.

21 R—Q6

21 . . . .   Q—KKt2 !

Smothering the counter-chances that result from 21 . . . P—K5; 22 P—B4 !, P × P; 23 B—R4 !, P—B6; 24 B × Kt, R × B; 25 R × R, P × B; 26 R—K1 and Black has no compensation for the lost exchange.

22 B—B1

22 B—K1 was somewhat better, although in that case 22 . . . P—B5 yields a strong attack (not 22 . . . P—K5; 23 B—B3 !).

22 . . . .   P—K5 !

Here the advance of the Pawn is formidable because 23 P × P is refuted by 23 . . . Kt × P; 24 R—Q7, Q × P etc.

23 B—K1   P × P
24 B—B3   Q—K2 !

(See diagram next column)

25 R(6)—Q3

Realizing somewhat tardily that if 25 B × Kt, Q × P ch; 26 K—R1, P × P ch; 27 B ×

P, Q—K8 ch ! and mate follows. Having missed this fine point, Vidmar is rightly pessimistic!

25 . . . .   P × P
26 B × P   B × B
27 B × Kt

Running into a catastrophe; but if 27 K × B, Q—K5 ch; 28 K—Kt1, Kt—Kt5 or . . . Q—Kt5 ch and White is pitifully helpless.

27 . . . .   Q—K5
28 R(1)—Q2   B—R6
29 B—B3   Q—Kt5 ch

And Black announced mate in two. Nimzovich's breezy play here is most attractive.

38. *Fighting Chess*

W^{E HAVE} already observed in Game 31 that a fighting
mood is often conducive to blunders. And when the
play is as complicated as in this game, the appearance of
mistakes becomes more likely. It is almost painfully embarrassing, in playing over such a game, to see how nervous
tension affects the quality of even the greatest masters'
moves. Going over such a game almost smacks of eaves-
dropping!

NIMZOINDIAN ATTACK

New York, 1927

WHITE: *A. Nimzovich*   BLACK: *Dr. A. Alekhine*

| 1 | Kt—KB3 | Kt—KB3 |
| 2 | P—QKt3 | P—Q3 |

Black wants to set up a
Pawn at K4 to break the diagonal of the fianchettoed Bishop.

| 3 | P—Kt3 | P—K4 |
| 4 | P—B4 | ! ? |

Few players would have the
daring not to stop the following advance by playing the orthodox 4 P—Q3.

| 4 . . . . | P—K5 |
| 5 Kt—R4 | ! ? |

Nimzovich was not the man
to shrink from strong meas-

ures. After 5 Kt—Q4, P—Q4;
6 P × P, Q × P; 7 P—K3, Q
—K4 his position would be
very bad.

5 . . . .   P—Q4

This advance is possibly pre-

[143

mature. 5 . . . B—K2 is certainly safe and sound.

6 P × P	Q × P

But this leads to trouble, as is to be expected. The Tournament Book recommends 6 . . . Kt × P and if 7 B—QKt2, B—K2!

7 Kt—QB3	Q—B3
8 P—K3!?	

Leaves a frightful-looking weakness at Q3. However, Nimzovich realizes that the fianchetto of his King Bishop is out of the question, KKt2 being reserved for his King Knight.

8	P—QR3

He has to parry the threat of B—Kt5.

9 B—QKt2	B—KKt5
10 B—K2	B × B
11 Kt × B	QKt—Q2

The weakness of White's Q3 appears more glaring than ever; but Nimzovich manages to escape unharmed.

12 QR—B1	Q—Kt3

This leads to difficulties;

144]

hence the Tournament Book suggests 12 . . . Kt—B4; 13 O—O, Q—Q2; 14 B × Kt, P × B with chances and weaknesses for both players.

13 O—O	B—Q3
14 P—B3!?	

Brings the game to a crisis. If Black plays passively, his opponent will obtain a powerful center. Hence Black goes in for a wild combination.

14	B—K4?!
15 B × B	Kt × B
16 P × P	Kt—Q6

But not 16 . . . Kt × P; 17 Q—B2 and Black is in trouble.

17 R—QB3	O—O—O

White's position is very difficult: if 18 Q—B2, Kt—QKt5 regaining the Pawn with a good game, or 18 Kt—Q4, R × Kt! with a strong game. But Nimzovich finds a way out.

18 Q—Kt1!	Kt × P!

Well played on both sides. Less good for Black would be 18 . . . Kt—B4; 19 P—Q3, Kt—R5; 20 P × Kt, Q × P ch; 21 K—R1!, Q × Kt; 22 KR—

B1, R—Q2; 23 Q—Kt6, Kt—
K1; 24 R—QKt1, Kt—Q3; 25
Q—R7 etc. with a winning at-
tack.

19 R × Kt   Kt × QP
20 R × R *ch*   R × R
21 Q—B5 *ch*   K—Kt1

Black has two Pawns (plus
pressure) for his piece. A difficult situation for both players!

22 R—K1

22 R—B1 was better, for
reasons that will soon be clear.

22 . . . .   Q × P *ch*
23 Q—B2   Q—Q6
24 Kt—B4

White's position is still uncomfortable.

24 . . . .   Q—QB6 ?

Not the best. After 24 . . .
Q—B7 *!* Black would have
won a third Pawn, increasing
White's troubles considerably.

25 R—K3 *!*   Q—B8 *ch*

Now it is too late to go after
the extra Pawn: 25 . . . Q—
R8 *ch;* 26 K—Kt2, Q × P *?;*
27 Kt—B3 and Black is helpless against 28 Kt—Q3.

26 K—Kt2   Q—B3 *ch*

At last White's homesick
Knight can return from exile!

27 Kt—B3   P—KKt4

27 . . . Kt × Kt; 28 Q × Kt,
R—Q7 *ch;* 29 R—K2, Q—B7
offers even better possibilities
of resistance.

28 Kt—Q3 *!*   Kt × Kt

Black is powerless to avoid
the exchange, for if 28 . . .
Kt—K5; 29 Kt(B3)—K5 *!* etc.

29 Q × Kt   Q—B7 *ch*
30 Kt—B2   P—KB4
31 R—K2   Q—B4
32 Kt—Q3   Q—Q5
33 Kt—K5   P—B5 *!*
34 Kt—B4 *!*   P × P ?

[145

Missing the point of Nimzo-vich's last move. The following simplification eases White's task.

35 R—Q2 !   Q—R1

If 35 . . . P—Kt5; 36 Q—K3 ! etc.

36 R × R ch   Q × R
37 P × P   Q—Q5
38 Q—B8 ch   K—R2
39 Q—B2   Q × Q ch
40 K × Q   P—KR4

The ending which follows is won for White, but it offers some instructive moments.

41 K—K3   P—B4

Against 41 . . . P—Kt4, Nimzovich intended 42 Kt—Q2, P—R5; 43 P—KKt4 !, P—R6 (the Tournament Book

answers 43 . . . P—B4 with 44 Kt—K4 !, P—R6; 45 K—B3, P—B5; 46 P × P, P × P; 47 K—Kt3, K—Kt3; 48 K × P, K—R4; 49 K—Kt3, K—Kt5; 50 K—B3, K—R6; 51 K—K3, K × P; 52 K—Q4, K—Kt6; 53 Kt—B5 ch etc.); 44 K—B3, P—B4; 45 Kt—K4, P—B5; 46 P—Kt4, K—Kt3; 47 K—Kt3 !, K—B3; 48 Kt × P !, P—B6; 49 Kt—B3 ! and wins.

42 P—R4   P—Kt4
43 P × P   P × P
44 Kt—Q2   K—Kt3

Black's last hope is to create a passed Pawn on either wing. But the Knight is too agile.

45 Kt—K4   P—R5
46 P—KKt4 !   P—R6
47 K—B3   P—Kt5

His last hope. If 47 . . . P—B5; 48 P—Kt4, K—B3; 49 Kt—B3 winning easily.

48 Kt × KtP   P—B5
49 Kt—K4   P × P

If 49 . . . P—B6; 50 Kt—B2, P—B7; 51 Kt—Q3 and wins.

50 P—Kt5   P—Kt7
51 Kt—Q2   K—B4

52	P—Kt6	P—R7
53	K—Kt2	K—Q5
54	P—Kt7	K—Q6
55	P—Kt8(Q)	K × Kt
56	Q—R2	K—B7
57	Q—B4 *ch*	Resigns

After 57 . . . K—Q7; 58 Q × P *ch*, K—B8; 59 Q—B3 *ch*, K—Kt8; 60 K × P, K—R8; 61 Q—R6 *ch* a standard book ending is reached. An inordinately difficult game! Both adversaries were out for blood.

39.   *The Pin is Mightier than the Sword*

STUDENTS of Nimzovich's theories are familiar with the emphasis he placed on the pin as a means of restraint and as a tactical weapon. It was a subject to which he had devoted much thought; the theme was one which he handled very skilfully in his games.

The following game illustrates Nimzovich's mastery of this motif. It features two pins; the first wins material, the second conclusively demolishes Black's position.

KING'S INDIAN DEFENSE

(in effect)

New York, 1927

(Third Brilliancy Prize)

WHITE: *A. Nimzovich*   BLACK: *F. J. Marshall*

1	P—QB4	Kt—KB3
2	P—Q4	P—K3
3	Kt—KB3	P—B4
4	P—Q5	P—Q3

From an aggressive player like Marshall, one would expect the Blumenfeld Counter Gambit (4 . . . P—QKt4). The text leads to a passive set-up

[147

which must have been agony to Marshall.

5 Kt—B3 P × P

This only gives White's pieces greater freedom. 5 . . . P—K4 is probably preferable.

6 P × P P—KKt3
7 Kt—Q2

The splendid square QB4 beckons to the Knight.

7 . . . . QKt—Q2

He must challenge the White KKt at once; for if 7 . . . B—Kt2; 8 Kt—B4, O—O; 9 B—B4 and Black cannot play . . . QKt—Q2.

8 Kt—B4 Kt—Kt3
9 P—K4 B—Kt2 ?

"In cramped positions, always exchange." 9 . . . Kt × Kt was in order.

10 Kt—K3 !

After this, Black's Queen Knight plays a miserable role throughout the game.

10 . . . . O—O
11 B—Q3 Kt—R4

Feeling uncomfortable in his crowded position, Marshall characteristically plays for attack—which, however, lacks every prospect of success. The Tournament Book recommends 11 . . . B—Q2; 12 O—O, Q —B2; 13 P—QR4, QR—K1; 14 P—R5, Kt—B1—which has the virtue of mobilizing Black's Queen-side forces.

12 O—O B—K4

Relatively better was 12 . . . Kt—B5. Black's attempt to attack will lead to a fiasco, as he cannot prevent P—B4 in the long run.

13 P—QR4 Kt—KB5
14 P—R5 Kt—Q2

Marshall is playing for one of his famous swindles: 15 B —B2, Q—R5; 16 P—KKt3, Q

—R6; 17 P × Kt *?*, B × P; 18 Kt—Kt4, Kt—K4 *!* drawing. But Nimzovich crosses this plan and brings the game to a critical stage.

15 Kt—B4 *!*

Now Black's priceless Bishop cannot retreat.

15 . . . .   Kt × B
16 Q × Kt   P—B4

He opens new lines—for his opponent. But 16 . . . B—Q5 would be answered by 17 B—K3 (not 17 Kt × P *?*, Kt—K4).

17 P × P   R × P
18 P—B4 *!*

18 Kt—K4 was simple and strong; but Nimzovich decides to force the issue, disregarding the weakness of his Queen's Pawn.

18 . . . .   B—Q5 *ch*

A finesse: the immediate 18 . . . B × Kt; 19 P × B, Kt—B3 would be catastrophic for Black: 20 Kt—K3 followed by 21 P—B4 and 22 B—Kt2 with a won game.

19 B—K3   B × Kt

20 Q × B *!*   Kt—B3

If 20 . . . R × QP; 21 Q—Kt3 *!* (21 P—B5 *!*, P × P; 22 R—B3 is also very strong), K—Kt2; 22 B—Q2 followed by 23 B—B3 *ch* and Black has a lost game.

21 Q—Kt3 *!*

21 . . . .   R × QP

If 21 . . . Kt × P; 22 QR—K1 *!* and Black is hopelessly tied up. He cannot play 22 . . . B—K3 because of 23 B × P. Nimzovich would have continued (say after 22 . . . R—B2) with 23 B—Q2 followed by the doubling of his Rooks on the King file. The rapid collapse of Black's game would then be a foregone conclusion.

Another powerful reply to
21 . . . Kt × P would have
been the simple 22 QR—Q1.

22 P—B5 !   P × P

22 . . . B × P; 23 B—Kt5,
R—Q6; 24 Q × P is also very
bad for Black.

23 B—Kt5 !

Black is two Pawns ahead,
but his position is hopeless.
Thus if 23 . . . K—Kt2; 24 Q
—Kt3 !, K—B2 (the threat was
25 B × Kt ch, K × B; 26 Q—
R4 ch); 25 QR—Q1 and the
attack must triumph. Or 23
. . . B—K3; 24 Q × P, R—B1
(if 24 . . . R—Kt1; 25 B × Kt
wins); 25 QR—K1 ! and Black
must lose a piece! A typically
subtle Nimzovich combination!
The best is yet to come.

23 . . . .   R—Q5
24 Kt—Kt6 ch P—B5
25 Q—QB3   P × Kt
26 Q × R   K—Kt2

If 26 . . . K—B2; 27 Q—
R4 wins quickly.

27 QR—K1 !

The shortest way. If now 27
. . . K—Kt3; 28 R—K8 ! is
crushing; if 27 . . . B—Q2;
28 B × Kt ch, Q × B; 29 R—
K7 ch etc.

27 . . . .   P × P

28 R—K8 !   Q × R
29 Q × Kt ch   K—Kt1
30 B—R6   Resigns

Mate is unavoidable. An
elegant game.

40. *White Magic*

T HE MAILED fist in the velvet glove" is the apt phrase for this game. Ahues, no mean tactician himself, is battered into submission by a series of moves which are elegant and subtle. His defeat is all the more crushing because Nimzovich's play here is so refined. We might think of Black's moves as a quiz on which Ahues did very badly!

NIMZOINDIAN DEFENSE

Berlin, 1927

WHITE: *K. Ahues*   BLACK: *A. Nimzovich*

1	P—Q4	Kt—KB3
2	P—QB4	P—K3
3	Kt—QB3	B—Kt5
4	B—Q2	O—O
5	Kt—B3	

Ahues is a natural player who avoids dogmatic opening lines. The drawback to this tame policy is that Black has an easy time of it from the very start.

5	P—QKt3
6 P—K3	

(*See diagram next column*)

6	B × Kt !

Trust Nimzovich not to miss

a fine point! After 6 . . . B—Kt2; 7 B—Q3, KB × Kt; 8 B × B, Kt—K5; 9 B × Kt *!*, B × B; 10 Kt—Q2 *!*, B—Kt2 (if 10 . . . B × P; 11 KR—Kt1 White has a strong attack); 11 Q—Kt4 White has a good attacking position. A game Tartakover—

Thomas (Scarborough, 1929)
continued 11 . . . P—Q3; 12
P—Q5 !, P—K4; 13 P—B4,
P—KB3; 14 O—O, R—B2 ?;
15 P × P, QP × P; 16 B × P !

7 B × B	Kt—K5
8 Q—B2	B—Kt2
9 O—O—O	

With Black's Bishop trained
on White's King-side, White
decides to seek safety on the
other wing.

| 9 . . . . | P—KB4 |
| 10 Kt—K5 ? | |

He wants to rid himself of
the annoying Knight, but his
development is sadly neglect-
ed. 10 B—Q3 was preferable.

10	Q—K2
11 P—B3	Kt × B
12 Q × Kt	P—Q3
13 Kt—Q3	Kt—Q2
14 K—Kt1 !	

Intending the temporary
sacrifice of a Pawn with P—
B5. Normal moves are already
at a premium (14 B—K2, P—
K4 ! with the better game).

But, as usual, Nimzovich
takes the initiative with a series of unexpected moves.

152]

| 14 . . . . | QR—Q1 ! |

Very sly. On 15 Q—R3
Nimzovich intends 15 . . . P
—QR4; 16 P—B5, QP × P;
17 P × P, Kt—K4 ! (not 17
. . . Kt × P because of the
counter-pin 18 R—B1 !) and
White cannot parry the double
threat of 18 . . . Kt × P ! or
18 . . . Kt—B5 ! (for example
18 R—B1, Kt × Kt; 19 B ×
Kt, Q—Kt4; 20 B—B1, R—
Q7 with a winning game).

| 15 P—KR4 ? | |

To prevent . . . Q—Kt4; but
15 B—K2, P—K4 was assur-
edly the lesser evil.

15	Q—B3
16 Q—R3	P—QR4
17 B—K2	P—K4 !

This leaves White little

choice, as he cannot afford to allow his weakness on the King's file to be uncovered.

18 P—Q5   P—B5 !
19 P—K4   Q—Kt3 !

White's King-side is badly crippled by the earlier advance of the King's Rook Pawn. The fact that Black's Bishop is out of the game is offset by the lack of cooperation among White's forces.

20 QR—Kt1   Kt—B3 !

Threatening to increase the pressure unbearably with . . . Kt—R4—Kt6. Nimzovich has provided against the counter-attack 21 P—B5 with the following ingenious variation: 21 . . . Kt—R4 *!;* 22 P—KKt4, P × P e.p.; 23 P × KtP, P × P; 24 Q—Kt3, B—R3; 25 Kt × P, P × Kt; 26 B × B, P—Kt7 and wins.

21 P—KKt3

A "cure" which proves just as bad as the disease.

21 . . . .   P × P
22 P—B5

22 . . . .   Kt × KP *!*

So that if 23 P × Kt, Q × P; 24 B—Q1 (if 24 B—B1, R × B *ch !* or 24 R—K1, P—Kt7; 25 KR—Kt1, QP × P winning easily), P—Kt7; 25 R—R2, B —R3; 26 B—B2, R—B8 *ch* and wins (Nimzovich).

23 P × KtP   Kt—Q7 *ch*

Now White's game crumbles: if 24 K—B2 (or 24 K—B1, Q—R3), Kt—B5; 25 Q—B3 (if 25 Q—Kt3, Kt—K6 *ch* and 26 . . . B × P), Kt—K6 *ch* and 26 . . . Kt × P.

24 K—R1   P × P
25 R—R3   P—Kt7

A nice possibility now is 26 R—R2, Kt × P; 27 R(2) × P (27 B × Kt, R × B; 28 R(2)

[153

× P, Q × R!), Kt × R; 28 R
× Q, P × R (28 ... Kt × B!
also wins easily); 29 B—Q1,
R—B8; 30 Q—Kt3, P—K5; 31
Kt—B1, R—QB1; 32 K—Kt1,
P—K6! and wins.

26	Q—B3	Q—R3
27	R × P	R—B1
28	Q—R3	Kt × P
29	R—R1	

Now 29 ... P—K5 wins a
piece, but Nimzovich selects
an even more sadistic way.

| 29 .... | B × P |

White resigns, for if 30 P—
Kt3 (to guard against ... P—
K5), Kt—Q5 wins a Rook! A
delectable game! Ahues has
been outgeneraled all the way.

41. "Appearance and Reality"

RELENTLESS critic of Nimzovich's play that he was, Tarrasch once remarked that his "ugly" moves were less
forgivable than outright blunders! Hans Kmoch, a more
discerning observer, wrote in moving terms of the loneli-
ness of the genius who is deprived of sympathetic appreciation, and has to make his way against ridicule and hostility.
Nimzovich brushed off Tarrasch's argument brusquely. "The
beauty of a chess move," he wrote, "lies not in its appearance, but in the thought behind it."

SICILIAN DEFENSE

Kecskemet, 1927

WHITE: *A. Nimzovich*   BLACK: *K. Gilg*

1	P—K4	P—QB4
2	Kt—KB3	Kt—QB3
3	B—Kt5	

The "ugly" move: ugly be-
cause unusual.

| 3 .... | Q—B2 |

Nimzovich prefers . . . P—Q3.

4 P—B3	P—QR3
5 B—R4	Kt—B3
6 Q—K2	

With the King Bishop developed, the text becomes feasible. White is ready to build an attractive Pawn center with P—Q4, which explains Black's reply.

6 . . . .   P—K4

Not good; the resulting opening up of the position will be catastrophic for Black.

| 7 O—O | B—K2 |
| 8 P—Q4 ! | |

Energetic play which poses a difficult problem for Black.

White's last move involved a Pawn sacrifice which is best declined by 8 . . . P—QKt4.

8 . . . .   BP × P

Also unsatisfactory is 8 . . . O—O; 9 B × Kt, Q × B; 10 P × KP, Kt × P (10 . . . Q × P; 11 Q × Q, Kt × Q; 12 R—K1 also loses a piece for Black); 11 R—K1, P—B4 (11 . . . P—Q4; 12 P × P e.p. loses a piece without any complications); 12 P × P c.p., Kt × P(3); 13 Q × B, R—K1; 14 Q × R ch, Kt × Q; 15 R × Kt ch, K—B2; 16 Kt—K5 ch and White has won a piece.

9 P × P	Kt × QP
10 Kt × Kt	P × Kt
11 P—K5 !	P—Q6

Or 11 . . . Kt—Q4; 12 P—K6, P × P; 13 Q × KP, Kt—Kt3; 14 B—KKt5 !, Q—Q1; 15 B × B, Kt × B; 16 Q—Kt3, Q × B; 17 Q × Kt (Nimzovich) with much the better game for White. Black is conducting middle game operations with his King in the center—always dangerous.

12 Q—K3 !

[155

12 . . . .   Kt—Q4

On 12 . . . B—B4 Nimzo-
vich intended 13 Q—Kt3, Kt
—K5; 14 Q × KtP, B × P *ch*;
15 K—R1 *!* (not 15 R × B *? ?*,
Q × B *ch* and wins), R—B1;
16 B—R6, B—B4; 17 P—K6 *!*

13 Q—Kt3   P—KKt3

If 13 . . . O—O; 14 B—R6
wins easily.

14 B—Kt3 *!*   Kt—Kt5

On 14 . . . Q—B3; 15 Q—
B3 *!* is a crushing reply.

15 B × P *ch !*   K—Q1

Forced: 15 . . . K × B *? ?*;
16 P—K6 *ch*.
Now White must guard
against . . . Kt—B7.

156]

16 B—R6 *!*

. . . But he doesn't!

16 . . . .   Kt—B7

Why not?!

17 Kt—B3   Kt—Q5

White's Rook is tainted: if
17 . . . Kt × R; 18 Kt—Q5,
Q—B3; 19 B—K3 *!*, P—Q3
(or 19 . . . B—B4; 20 Q—
Kt5 *ch*); 20 B—Kt6 *ch*, K—
Q2; 21 P—K6 mate!

18 Q × QP   Q × P
19 KR—K1   Q—B3
20 R × B *!*   Resigns

If 20 . . . K × R; 21 Kt—
Q5 *ch*. Or 20 . . . Q × R; 21
Q × Kt attacking the Rook
while threatening Q—Kt6
mate.

42. *Fourth Dimension*

THE GREAT masters have chess in their fingertips. They know how to produce games that dazzle us with the vivid contrast of thrust and counter-thrust. The great writers on chess love to annotate such games; they are fond of dramatizing the pieces, which take on lifelike qualities.

"Reti has said," Fine notes in *Chess Marches On*, "that the combination represents the triumph of mind over matter. There is no doubt that his judgment shows real insight. The combination, the sacrifice, the unexpected turn imbue the wooden pieces with sparkle, almost make them come to life. 'This Bishop,' writes Lasker in his annotations to a position, 'smiles.' 'The other Bishop,' he continues, 'laughs.'"

Nimzovich, as anyone who is familiar with his games can testify, had this knack of the dramatic. But he not only breathed life into the pieces: he even brought the very squares of the chessboard to life in a way that reminds us irresistibly of the old Pygmalion legend.

SICILIAN DEFENSE

London, 1927

(Prize for the best-played game)

WHITE: *F. D. Yates*   BLACK: *A. Nimzovich*

1 P—K4	P—QB4

with another defense.

"Fe, fi, fo, fum, I smell the blood of an Englishman." Having played the French with success against Yates in Game 34, Nimzovich tries his luck

2 Kt—KB3	Kt—KB3
3 P—K5	Kt—Q4
4 B—B4	

Tame; more forceful is 4 P —Q4 or 4 Kt—B3.

[157

4	Kt—Kt3
5 B—K2	Kt—B3
6 P—B3	P—Q4
7 P—Q4	

7 P × P e.p., Q × P gives
Black a good development.

7	P × P
8 P × P	B—B4
9 O—O	P—K3

Black is developing his game
efficiently and effortlessly—an
indication that White's opening play has not been energetic
enough.

| 10 Kt—B3 | B—K2 |
| 11 Kt—K1 | |

Nimzovich criticizes White's
plan, recommending B—K3
followed by R—B1, P—QR3,
P—QKt4 and Kt—Q2—Kt3—
B5.

| 11 . . . . | Kt—Q2 ! |

So that if 12 P—B4 ?, Kt ×
QP !; 13 Q × Kt ? ?, B—B4.

12 B—Kt4 !

If 12 B—K3, Kt(2) × P !;
13 P × Kt, P—Q5 simplifying
advantageously.

158]

12	B—Kt3
13 P—B4	Kt × QP
14 Kt × P !	Kt—QB3 !

A sharp skirmish between
two master tacticians. If 14
. . . P × Kt; 15 B × Kt *ch*, Q
× B; 16 Q × Kt etc.

| 15 Kt × B | Q—Kt3 *ch* |
| 16 K—R1 | Kt × Kt |

P—B5 is still restrained.

17 Q—R4 ?

Instead of this *decentralization* he should have guarded
the center with 17 Q—K2.

| 17 . . . . | P—KR4 ! |
| 18 B—R3 | |

If 18 B—B3, Kt—B4 with
the nasty menace of . . . P—
R5 and . . . Kt—Kt6 *ch*.

| 18 . . . . | B—B4 ! |
| 19 Q—R3 | Q—Kt4 ! |

Gaining time to maneuver a Knight to Q4.

| 20 K—Kt1 | Kt—QKt3 |
| 21 Q—KB3 | Kt(3)—Q4 |

He handles the Knights with his usual skill. Observe how the important play continually shapes up on the white squares.

| 22 P—QKt3 | Q—Kt3 ch |
| 23 R—B2 | |

| 23 . . . . | QR—B1 |

Not the best, says Nimzovich; he recommends 23 . . . O—O—O; 24 B—R3, B—Kt5 !; 25 R—B1 ch, K—Kt1; 26 B—B5, Q × B; 27 R × Q, B × Q; 28 R × B, R—QB1—or 23 . . . B—Kt5 !; 24 B × B, P × B; 25 Q × P, R × P; 26 Q × KtP, O—O—O with a winning game in either case.

24 B—Q2	R—R3 !
25 R—Q1	B × B
26 Q × B	Kt—B4

With the disappearance of White's white-squared Bishop, Black's control of these squares has been emphasized; note that P—KKt4 has been neutralized by 24 . . . R—R3 !

27 Q—Q3	R—Kt3
28 Kt—B3	R—Kt5
29 P—KR3	R—Kt6

The failure to castle has done Black no harm; he has good prospects for the middle game or ending.

| 30 P—QR4 | Kt—R5 |
| 31 K—B1 | R—B3 ! |

Forestalling danger by way of Q—R7.

32 P—R5	Q—Q1
33 K—Kt1	Kt—B4
34 K—R2	P—R3
35 Q—Kt1	Q—K2 !

[159

Provoking White's reply (best is 36 R—QB1, with a long struggle in prospect).

36 Kt—Q4 ?   Q—R5 !

With the terrible threat of mate beginning with 37 . . . R × RP *ch !*

37 B—K1

Forced—but inadequate.

37 . . . .   Kt × P

Now he threatens mate by way of 38 . . . R × KtP *ch !* etc.

38 R × Kt   R × RP *ch !*
39 P × R   Q × R *ch*
40 K—Kt2

If 40 K—R1, Kt × Kt wins quickly.

40 . . . .   Kt—K6 *ch !*

White resigns, as he cannot avoid mate in two.

This was one of **Nimzovich's** most difficult games.

43.   *Bogo Stubs His Toe*

TO PLAY for the attack consistently in master tournaments, one must have a resolute and sanguine temperament—in short, one must be an optimist. Bogolyubov is the ideal example of the optimist. If he wins, the critics sing hosannas about his marvellous attacking ability. If he loses, they damn his lack of self-discipline.

In this game, we see the seamy side of Bogolyubov's optimism. He starts out with a puerile wing demonstration which is convincingly refuted by Nimzovich. Move by move, the system is applied with schoolmasterish precision and cumulative effect. Bogolyubov must have blushed!

ENGLISH OPENING

London, 1927

WHITE: *E. Bogolyubov*   BLACK: *A. Nimzovich*

1 P—QB4	P—K3
2 Kt—QB3	Kt—KB3
3 P—K4	P—B4

Not fearing 4 P—K5, which is answered by 4 . . . Kt—Kt1 and 5 . . . P—Q3, when the advanced Pawn cannot be maintained.

4 P—KKt3	P—Q4
5 P—K5	P—Q5

The counterthrust equalizes.

6 P × Kt	P × Kt
7 QP × P	

Both this move and 7 KtP × P leave White with a theoretically dubious Pawn structure. However, the alternative 7 BP × P, P × P *ch;* 8 B × P, B × P leaves Black with an easy game.

7	Q × P
8 Kt—B3	P—KR3

To avoid the embarrassing move 9 B—Kt5. Having been developed early in the game, Black's Queen is subject to attack by White's minor pieces.

9 B—Kt2	B—Q2 *!*

Immediately taking steps to neutralize the long diagonal.

10 Kt—Q2	B—B3

Simple and good.

11 Kt—K4	Q—Kt3 *!*

Somewhat risky, but Nimzovich has calculated well. If White tries to parry the "threat" of 12 . . . P—B4 with 12 Kt—Q6 *ch,* there follows 12 . . . B × Kt; 13 B × B *ch,* Kt × B; 14 Q × B, Q—K5 *ch* and wins.

The early Queen moves make a dubious impression, but Nimzovich has accurately appraised the situation.

[161

| 12 Q—K2 ! | B—K2 ! |

12 . . . P—B4 is answered
by 13 B—B3 ! (threatening to
win the Queen with 14 B—
R5), followed by 14 Kt—Q2
and Black has no compensation
for his weakened center.

| 13 O—O | O—O |
| 14 P—KR4 ? | |

An optimistic advance which
is brutally repulsed. White
wants to exploit the apparently exposed position of the hostile Queen, and in doing so, he
sets some sly traps. But the
only result is that he weakens
his Pawn position fatally. Better was 14 P—B4, Kt—Q2; 15
B—Q2 with about an even
game. But Bogolyubov lacks
the necessary self-control.

| 14 . . . . | P—B4 |
| 15 Kt—Q2 | B × B ! |

If 15 . . . B × P; 16 Kt—
B3 !, B—K2 ! (not 16 . . . P
× Kt ?; 17 Q × B and wins);
17 Kt—K5, Q—B3; 18 B × B
and after 18 . . . P × B the
extra Pawn is outweighed by
Black's miserable Pawn structure.

| 16 K × B | Kt—B3 ! |

If 16 . . . B × P; 17 Kt—
B3, B—K2; 18 R—K1, R—
B3; 19 B—B4 with a powerful
grip on the position. So the
Pawn offer is best declined.

| 17 Kt—B3 | P—B5 ! |

The refutation of 14 P—
KR4 ? The text exploits the
weakness created in White's

Pawn position and prevents B —B4, which would guard the weakness and exert pressure on K5.

| 18 R—K1 | R—B3 |
| 19 Q—K4 | |

Or 19 Kt—K5, Kt × Kt; 20 Q × Kt, QR—KB1 with a powerful attack.

| 19 . . . . | P × P |

If now 20 Q × Q, R × Q; 21 P × P, B—Q3 and wins.

20 P × P	B—Q3
21 P—KKt4	Q × Q
22 R × Q	QR—KB1

The exchange of Queens has not diminished the virulence of Black's attack.

| 23 R—K3 | R—B5 |
| 24 P—Kt5 | |

Or 24 R × P, R × P *ch* and wins.

| 24 . . . . | R—Kt5 *ch* |
| 25 K—R1 | |

If 25 K—B2, Kt—K4; 26 K —K2, R—Kt7 *ch;* 27 K—B1, R—Kt6 winning easily.

| 25 . . . . | P × P |

25 . . . R—Kt6; 26 Kt— R2, R—B7 is another way.

| 26 P × P | K—B2 *!* |
| 27 Kt—Kt1 | R—R1 *ch* |

If now 28 R—R3 *?*, R× Kt *ch.*

28 Kt—R3	K—K2 *!*
29 P—Kt3	B—B5
30 R—B3	Kt—K4 *!*

White resigns, ruinous loss of material being unavoidable. His Queen-side forces cut an inglorious figure!

44. "It Was Planned That Way"

THE GAMES of most players leave us dissatisfied: the play is improvised, hit-or-miss, incoherent. The games of the great masters, on the other hand, give us pleasure because they generally embody the execution of a plan. To follow the conception and execution of a far-reaching plan is enjoyable because it gives us an intimation of man's attempts to impose order on a chaotic universe.

Nimzovich's games are particularly rich in this kind of satisfaction, for his system frequently dictates the *a priori* considerations which comprise the appropriate plan in a given position.

ENGLISH OPENING

London, 1927

(Imperial Chess Club Tournament)

WHITE: *V. Buerger*   BLACK: *A. Nimzovich*

1	P—QB4	Kt—KB3
2	Kt—QB3	P—B4
3	P—KKt3	P—KKt3
4	B—Kt2	B—Kt2

Such symmetrical formations often wind up in a shadow-boxing bout; but not when Nimzovich is one of the players!

5	P—Q3	O—O
6	B—Q2	P—K3
7	Q—B1	P—Q4

Both sides have formulated their plans in a paradoxical

manner. White is using hypermodern strategy (pressure on
the center from the wings);
Black is using classical strategy: occupation of the center
with Pawns. Has Nimzovich
deserted his system? The answer is "No!" He foresees that
White's plan will fail because
his pieces lack scope.

8 Kt—R3

Or 8 B—R6, P—Q5; 9 B ×
B (on 9 Kt—Q1, Q—R4 *ch* is
annoying), K × B; 10 Kt—Q1,
P—K4 and Black has a good
game. The text avoids blocking the long diagonal.

8	P—Q5
9 Kt—R4	Kt—R3
10 P—QR3	

White wants to gain space
on the Queen's wing with P—
QKt4.

10	Q—K1
11 P—Kt3	P—K4
12 Kt—Kt2	B—Kt5

To prevent White from
castling. 13 B × P? would
now be a mistake because of
13 . . . B × Kt; 14 B × Kt,
Q—B3 etc.

13 Kt—Kt5 !	R—Kt1
14 P—Kt4	P—Kt3
15 P—Kt5	Kt—B2
16 P—QR4	B—B1 !

The power of White's fianchettoed Bishop must be neutralized.

17 P—R5	B—Kt2

18 P—B3 ? !

A courageous move. 18 B ×
B, R × B; 19 P × P, P × P
was simple and good, but
Black would react strongly
with an eventual . . . P—K5.
White remains faithful to the
spirit of his thirteenth move,
and tries to restrain the advance in the center.

18	Kt—K3
19 P—R6 ?	

White clings to his plan. Again 19 P × P was better, in order to keep Black preoccupied with a possible R—R7. But who could expect Nimzovich's reply?!

19 . . . .   **B—QR1 ! !**

Nimzovich never lacked the courage of his convictions. He stalemates the Bishop, serenely awaiting the ultimate feasibility of . . . P—K5.

20 P—R4 ?

Leads to a serious weakening of his King-side Pawns; Kt —Q1—B2 was by far preferable.

20 . . . .   **Kt—R4 !**
21 Kt × Kt   **Q × Kt**

Now Black is ready for . . . P—B4.

22 P—Kt4   **Kt—B3**
23 B—R3   **Q—Q3**
24 Kt—Q1   **P—R4 !**

Forcing White to commit himself.

25 P—Kt5   **Kt—R2**
26 Kt—B2   **P—B3 !**

If now 27 KR—Kt1, P—B4 followed by the decisive break . . . P—K5 after due preparation.

27 P × P   **KB × P**
28 B—Kt5   **B × B**
29 P × B   **R—B5 !**

The weakened black squares are welcome targets for Nimzovich.

30 KR—Kt1   **QR—KB1**

Much stronger than winning a Pawn by . . . Q—K2 etc.

31 B—B1   **R—R5 !**

So that if 32 Kt—R3, P—K5 !; 33 QP × P, Q—R7 wins.

32 Q—Q2   **R—R7 !**

Preventing White from castling. The annoying Rook must be removed.

33 R—Kt2   **R × R**
34 B × R   **P—K5 ! !**

At last. This is the breakthrough for which Nimzovich has been warily waiting for so many moves. Its effect is decisive.

35 QP × P

If 35 Kt × P, B × Kt; 36 QP × B, Q—Kt6 *ch;* 37 K—B1, Kt × P; 38 Q—K1 (or 38 K—Kt1, R × P), Q—R7 *!* and wins.

35 . . . .   Q—Kt6
36 K—B1

Or 36 B—B1, B × P with an easy win.

36 . . . .   Kt × P

Intending to answer 37 Kt—R1 with . . . Kt × KP *!*

37 K—Kt1   R × P *!*

Another way was 37 . . . P—R5; 38 Kt—R1, Kt—R6 *ch;* 39 K—B1, Q—R7; 40 B ×

Kt, Q × Kt *ch;* 41 K—B2, Q × B (on 41 . . . Q × R; 42 Q—R6 is annoying) with an easy win.

38 Q × Kt

He has no choice, 38 Q—K1 or R—KB1 being answered by 38 . . . R × Kt.

38 . . . .   Q × Q
39 P × R   Q—K6
40 R—Q1   Q—Kt6
41 R—QB1   P—Kt4 *!*

White's pieces are still huddled together ineffectually.

42 K—R2   Q—K6
43 R—B1   Q—K7
44 Kt—R3   P—Q6
45 Kt—B2   P—Q7
46 K—Kt1   Q × QBP
47 R—Q1   Q—B8
48 B—R3   P—Kt5
49 P × P   B × P

Freedom! The Bishop will provide the finishing touch.

50 P × P   B—B6

White resigns. An absorbing game.

45. *Seeing Things*

NIMZOVICH's style, directed always toward the profound and the unusual, predisposed him to the danger of making serious oversights. Sometimes, as in this game, his trouble was that in search of the perfect win, he overlooked the simple lines of play.

QUEEN'S PAWN OPENING

Carlsbad, 1929

WHITE: *Dr. M. Vidmar* BLACK: *A. Nimzovich*

1	P—Q4	Kt—KB3
2	Kt—KB3	P—K3
3	B—Kt5	

A harmless continuation favored by old-fashioned players to whom the thought of an Indian Defense is repulsive.

3	. . . .	P—B4
4	P—K3	Q—Kt3
5	Q—B1	Kt—B3
6	P—B3	P—Q4

Black already has some initiative, plus an easy development.

7	B—Q3	B—Q3
8	QKt—Q2	P × P *!*
9	KP × P	

This weakens his KB4, but the alternative 9 BP × P is answered too strongly by 9 . . . Kt—QKt5.

9	. . . .	Kt—KR4 *!*

White is hardly in a position to dispute the coming occupation of his KB4, for 10 P—

168]

KKt3 would create a serious King-side weakness for later exploitation by Black.

10 Kt—B1	P—KR3
11 B—Q2	Q—B2
12 Kt—Kt3	

Or 12 P—KKt3, P—K4; 13 P × P, Kt × KP and White's game has been badly compromised for King-side castling.

| 12 . . . . | Kt—B5 |
| 13 B × Kt | B × B |

Now Nimzovich has the two Bishops, and he employs them to good advantage later on.

| 14 Q—Q1 | P—KKt3 |

Beginning the familiar process of hemming in the Knights (Kt—R5 is prevented). In the sequel they play a pitiable role.

15 O—O	P—KR4
16 R—K1	O—O
17 Q—K2	K—Kt2

He decides that the Rook will be very useful at KR1 after all.

| 18 QR—Q1 |

Too much preparation: he should make the most of his best chance of counter-play by the immediate 18 Kt—K5.

18	R—R1 !
19 Kt—B1	P—R5
20 Kt—K5 ?	Kt × Kt
21 P × Kt	R—R4

Winning the King Pawn in broad daylight. Now we can see that Vidmar's play was badly timed.

| 22 P—KKt3 | R × P |
| 23 Q—B3 | R—Kt4 ! |

Keeping the King's Bishop on his best diagonal. In addition to his plus Pawn, Nimzovich will soon have a devastating attack.

24 K—R1	P × P
25 BP × P	B—Q3
26 R—Q2	B—Q2
27 R—KB2	P—B4 !

The further advance of this Pawn will add fuel to the attack.

28 Q—K3	R—Kt5
29 Q—K2	R—R1
30 K—Kt1	B—B3

Nimzovich later pointed out

that in this classic attacking position he had an equally attractive continuation in 30 . . . P—Q5 !; 31 P × P, B—B3, for example 32 Kt—K3 (the threat was 32 . . . B × P !; 33 Kt × B, R × Kt ch), R × P ch !; 33 K—B1, R(6)—R6 winning easily.

| 31 Kt—K3 | R—Kt4 |
| 32 Kt—Kt2 | P—B5 ! |

Beginning the decisive attack.

33 P × P	B × P
34 K—B1	R × P
35 Q—B3	P—Q5 !
36 B—K4	

This loses, but he has no good move: if 36 Q × KB, B × Kt ch; 37 K—K2, Q × Q; 38 R × Q, B—K5 ch etc.

36 . . . .   R—KB4 ! ?

In calculating the far-reaching consequences of this fine move, Nimzovich completely overlooked the easier win beginning with 36 . . . R—R8 ch: 37 K—K2, B × B; 38 Q × KB (if 38 Q × QB, R—K4), Q —B5 ch; 39 K—Q1 (if 39 K— Q2, Black mates in three), Q —Q6 ch; 40 Q—Q2, Q × Q ch; 41 K × Q, R × Kt and Black is a piece to the good.

37 Q—Kt4

If 37 B × B, B—Kt6 wins wholesale. The position is full of pretty possibilities.

37	R—R8 ch
38 K—K2	R × R ch
39 K × R	B—Kt6
40 B × R	Q—K4 ch !
41 K—B1	

Still making forced moves; if 41 Q—K2 (or 41 K—Q1, P × B; 42 Q—K2, Q × Q ch; 43 R × Q, B—B6; 44 P × P, P— B5 !; 45 K—Q2, B × R; 46 K × B, K—B3 with an easily won ending), Q × B; 42 K— B1, Q × R ch likewise forcing a won King and Pawn ending.

41	P × B
42 P × P	

An amusing variation pointed out by Nimzovich is 42 Q—K2, B—Kt4 *!;* 43 P—B4, Q × Q *ch;* 44 R × Q (or 44 K × Q, B × P *ch* with an easy win), B × P and the Rook is pinned all over again! An example of humor in chess.

42	B × R
43 K × B	P × Q
44 P × Q	B × Kt
45 K × B	K—B2

The ending is an elementary book win, as Black's outside passed Pawn is decisive.

46 K—Kt3	K—K3
47 K × P	K × P
48 K—Kt5	K—K5
49 K × P	K—Q6
50 K—B5	K—B7
51 P—Kt4	P—Kt4

Choosing the hard way, which almost makes it seem close. 51 . . . K—Kt7 wins both White Pawns.

52 K—K5	K—B6
53 K—Q5	K × P
54 K—B6	P—R4
55 K—Kt6	P—R5
56 K—R6	P—R6
57 K—Kt6	K—B5
58 K—R5	P—Kt5
59 K—R4	K—B6

White resigns, for . . . P—Kt6 wins quickly.

46. "In Praise of Folly"

EXPERIENCE," says Josh Billings, "inkreases our wizdum but don't reduse our phollys." In Game 43, Bogolyubov had the sad experience of running afoul of Nimzovich's masterly exploitation of Pawn weaknesses. Learning nothing and forgetting nothing, Bogolyubov repeats his mistake.

NIMZOINDIAN DEFENSE

Carlsbad, 1929

(Prize for the best-played game)

WHITE: *E. Bogolyubov* BLACK: *A. Nimzovich*

1 P—Q4	Kt—KB3
2 P—QB4	P—K3
3 Kt—QB3	B—Kt5
4 Kt—B3	B × Kt *ch*

Nimzovich immediately accepts the invitation to give White a doubled Pawn.

5 P × B   P—QKt3

In Game 48, Nimzovich varied with 5 . . . P—Q3, which is even more effective.

6 P—KKt3

Weak: he should play 6 P—K3—or even 6 B—Kt5, B—Kt2; 7 Kt—Q2.

6	B—Kt2
7 B—KKt2	O—O
8 O—O	R—K1 *!*

Those "mysterious" Rook moves!

White's strategy calls for

172]

playing P—K4 *and keeping his other center Pawn at Q4.* However, if now 9 Kt—Q2, B × B; 10 K × B, P—K4 *!* and 11 P—K4 *?* loses a Pawn.

9 R—K1	P—Q3

Again, if now 10 Kt—Q2, B × B; 11 K × B, P—K4; 12 P—K4, Kt—B3 *!* and White's Pawn cannot be maintained at Q4 unless White wishes to resort to the awkward B—Kt2.

10 Q—B2	B—K5
11 Q—Kt3	Kt—B3
12 B—B1	

In order to play Kt—Q2 without exchanging Bishops. After 12 Kt—Q2, B × B; 13 K × B, Black could effectively play 13 . . . P—K4 or even 13 . . . P—Q4 *!*

12	P—K4 *!*
13 P × P *?*	

The losing move, as it leaves White with a doubled and isolated Queen's Bishop Pawn. For better or worse, he had to try 13 P—Q5, although it would have left Black with an appreciably superior game.

13	Kt × P *!*

Simplification is Black's trump card.

14 Kt × Kt	R × Kt
15 B—B4	R—K1
16 P—B3	B—Kt2
17 QR—Q1	Kt—Q2
18 P—K4	Q—B3

White seems to have obtained a game of sorts, but his Bishops are useless and his Pawn position is riddled with weaknesses. As soon as Black succeeds in playing the move called for by the system (. . . P—KB4) the whole flimsy structure will collapse.

19 B—Kt2	Kt—K4
20 R—Q2	R—K2
21 R(1)—Q1	B—B3

Consolidation: he rules out the remotest possibility of P—B5.

22 R—KB2	QR—K1
23 B—KB1 *? !*	P—KR3

Conscious of his superiority, Nimzovich avoids the possibly premature win of a Pawn by 23 . . . Kt × P *ch;* 24 R × Kt, P—KKt4; 25 R—B2, P × B; 26 R × BP, Q—Kt3 etc.

[173

24 B—K2	K—R1
25 Q—R3	Q—K3 *!*
26 Q—B1	

Desperately hoping to get the Queen back into play (not 26 Q × RP *? ?*, R—R1) and intending to answer 26 . . . Kt × P; 27 B × Kt, Q × B with 28 B × RP.

26	P—B4 *!*

At last. Now further weaknesses are uncovered.

27 P × P	Q × KBP
28 Q—Q2	Q—B2
29 Q—Q4	

After 29 B × Kt, R × B followed by . . . R—K6 the pressure on White's position would be intolerable. But there is more than one way to skin a cat.

174]

29	Kt—Kt3 *!*

Decisive, as it forces another set of doubled and isolated Pawns.

30 B—Q3	Kt × B
31 Q × Kt	Q × Q
32 P × Q	R—KB1

Another way was 32 . . . R—K6; 33 K—Kt2, R × P; 34 R × R, R—K6 etc.

33 P—KB5	B—Q2
34 R(1)—Q2	B × P
35 R(B2)—K2	R × R

Also good was 35 . . . R (2)—B2 etc.

36 B × R	R—K1
37 K—B2	R—K4

Threatening . . . R—R4—6.

38 R—Q5	P—KKt4
39 R × R	P × R
40 P—B5	

Else Black's King marches to QB4.

40	P × P
41 B—R6	P—K5 *!*

Creating a potential passed Pawn on the King-side.

42	P—QR4	K—Kt2
43	P—R5	P × P
44	K × P	K—B3
45	K—K3	K—K4

| 46 | B—B4 | B—Kt5 ! |

Preparing the advance of the King-side Pawns.

47	B—R6	P—R4
48	B—B4	P—R5
49	B—R6	B—Q8
50	B—Kt7	P—Kt5

White resigns, for after 51 B—B6, P—Kt6; 52 P × P, P × P; 53 B—Kt7, B—Kt6 ! there follows . . . B—Q4 and . . . P—Kt7 and the invasion by Black's King is assured.

47. Genius Conquers Theory

MANY of Nimzovich's victories were the result of his exploiting hostile weaknesses; some of his victories were achieved despite the existence of *the very same weaknesses in his own camp!* It reminds one of Samuel Butler's casuist:

> "He could distinguish and divide
> A hair 'twixt south and south-west side;
> On either which he would dispute,
> Confute, change hands, and still confute."

It is a situation which has ironic overtones, giving some point to the claims of Nimzovich's enemies that he won his games despite the "system," and not because of it! System or no system, the personal equation still plays a great role

[175

in chess; even if automata are perfected some day to replace humans in chess tournaments, one suspects that these machines will be in need of some irrational qualities!

DUTCH DEFENSE

Carlsbad, 1929

WHITE: *P. Johner*   BLACK: *A. Nimzovich*

1 P—Q4	P—KB4

Doubtless intending to answer the customary 2 P—KKt3 with 2 . . . P—Q3 etc. (see Game 32).

2 P—K4	P × P
3 Kt—QB3	Kt—KB3
4 B—KKt5	P—QKt3

This unusual counter to the Staunton Gambit was a favorite with Nimzovich.

5 P—B3	P—K6 *!*

He has no intention of giving White a big lead in development and good attacking chances by playing 5 . . . P × P.

We are at one of those crucial cross-roads where a game is virtually decided in the opening. A wrong choice now will spoil White's game irretrievably.

6 B × P *?*

Too hackneyed. Nimzovich recommends 6 Q—B1, but 6 P—Q5 *!* is even stronger, as it impedes Black's development and leaves him with a repulsive Pawn structure.

6	P—K3
7 Q—Q2	P—Q4 *! ?*

Giving himself a backward King's Pawn. However, the move is less objectionable than it seems at first sight: Black cannot avoid some Pawn weakness in the center, and the text at least gives Black the makings of a solid Pawn phalanx.

8 O—O—O   P—B4
9 B—Kt5 *ch*

Another banal move. A more promising plan is 9 P—B4 followed by 10 Kt—B3, 11 P—KKt3 and 12 B—R3.

9 . . . .   B—Q2
10 B × B *ch*   Q × B

It must be admitted that White's reasoning is attractive: he has deprived the King's Pawn of its protective Bishop.

11 Kt—R3

The originally intended 11 P—B4 is answered by 11 . . . P—B5 *!;* 12 Kt—B3(or 12 P—QR3, P—QKt4 *!* with sinister attacking intentions), B—Kt5 *!;* 13 Kt—K5, Q—QB2 followed by . . . Kt—K5.

11 . . . .   Kt—B3
12 KR—K1   O—O—O
13 Q—K2   P—B5 *!*
14 B—B4

Continuing to pile up on the

weak Pawn. White's moves are all taken out of the best elementary treatises, yet . . . they fail!

14 . . . .   R—K1

Black's game is as solid as the rock of ages. If 15 Kt—QKt5, Kt—KR4 *!* or 15 Kt—KKt5, B—Kt5 *!;* 16 Kt × KP *? ?,* Kt—Q1 etc.

15 Q—K3   P—KR3

And now if 16 Kt—QKt5, Kt—KR4 *!;* 17 Kt—B7 *?,* Kt × B; 18 Kt × R, Kt × Kt wins.

16 Kt—K2   P—QKt4 *!*
17 B—K5   B—Kt5 *!*

This sly move provokes White's reply, as he wants to keep his Rook on the King file.

18 P—B3   B—R4
19 B × Kt ?   P × B
20 Kt(2)—B4   P—Kt5 !

Pouncing on the target; and he has . . . P—K4 in reserve!

21 R—K2

Or 21 P × P (if 21 Kt × KP ?, P × P; 22 P × P, Kt—Q1; 23 Kt(3)—B4, B—B2 ! winning a piece), B × P; 22 R—K2, P—K4 ! with a winning game.

21 . . . .   P × P
22 P × P   Q—Q3

Beginning the final attack.

23 R—Kt2   Q—R6
24 Kt—K2   P—K4 !

Look at the lowly King's Pawn! White has no choice now: if 25 Q—Q2, Kt × P ! or 25 Q—B2, P × P etc.

25 P × P   R × P
26 Q—B2

Or 26 Q—Q2, P—Q5 !
With his usual diabolical energy, Nimzovich has snatched the initiative from his opponent. Johner is now taught a hard lesson.

26 . . . .   KR—K1 !

Much stronger than 26 . . . B × P; 27 Kt × B, Q × Kt ch; 28 Q—B2 etc.

27 Kt(3)—B4   B × P
28 Kt × B   Q × Kt ch

Now White must not play 29 Q—B2 because of 29 . . . Q—K6 ch !; 30 Q—Q2, P—B6 ! Or 29 R—B2, Q—R8 ch; 30 K—Q2, P—B6 ch !; 31 R × P, Q—Kt7 ch; 32 R—B2, Q—Kt5 ch; 34 K—Q3, Q × Kt; 35 R × Kt ch, K—Kt1; 36 R—Kt1 ch, K—R1 and wins!

29 K—Kt1   R—K8
30 R—Q2   R × R ch
31 R × R   R—K2 !
32 R—Q2

If 32 Q—B2, R—Kt2 ch; 33

K—B1, Q—R6 *ch* wins the
Queen.

32 . . . .   Q—Kt5 *ch !*

So that if 33 K—B2 (on 33
K—R1 or 33 K—B1, P—B6 *!*
wins), Q—R5 *ch;* 34 K—B3,
R—K6 *ch !* wins.

33 R—Kt2   R—K8 *ch*
34 K—B2   Q—R5 *ch*

White resigns, for if 35 K—
Q2, Q—Q8 *ch;* 36 K—B3, Q
—B8 *ch;* 37 Q—B2, R—K6
ch and mate next move. A
game which blends humor,
philosophy and instruction.

48. *Shaky Pawns*

MATTISON apes Bogolyubov's mistakes in Game 46 with
a steadfastness that is worthy of a better cause: he
weakens his Pawn position, fails to guard his weaknesses,
neglects opportunities for counterplay.

Nimzovich seizes every chance, and in the final phase he
deploys his Knights with the skill for which he was famous.
In a technical sense, it is interesting to watch his exploitation of the weakness of White's QB4—even when White's
shaky Pawn departs from that square.

NIMZOINDIAN DEFENSE

Carlsbad, 1929

WHITE: *H. Mattison*   BLACK: *A. Nimzovich*

1 P—Q4	Kt—KB3	
2 P—QB4	P—K3	
3 Kt—QB3	B—Kt5	
4 Kt—B3	B × Kt *ch*	

He loses no time in creating
the doubled Pawn "complex."

5 P × B	P—Q3
6 Q—B2	Q—K2

[179

7 B—R3

The Bishop is to exert pressure along the diagonal. . . . P—K4 is prevented, and White threatens to undouble with P—B5.

7 . . . .   P—B4
8 P—Kt3

Depriving his weak Pawn of support. Better was 8 P—K3, or else 8 P—K4, P—K4; 9 P—Q5.

8 . . . .   P—QKt3
9 B—KKt2   B—Kt2
10 O—O   O—O

Black stands well. He can look forward to attacking the weak Queen's Bishop Pawn, which has been fixed by 7 . . . P—B4.

11 Kt—R4

In order to challenge Black's power on the diagonal, and also to remove a potential menace (the hostile Bishop) to his Queen's Bishop Pawn.

But Nimzovich has indicated a stronger (centralizing!) line: 11 Kt—Q2 !, B × B; 12 K × B, Kt—B3; 13 P—K4 !, P × P; 14 P × P, Kt × QP; 15 Q—Q3, P—K4; 16 P—B4 with excellent counterplay for the Pawn. Nimzovich would not have accepted the Pawn sacrifice, but Mattison would have been much better off than in the actual play.

11 . . . .   B × B
12 K × B ?

It was vital to bring the Knight away from the side of the board: 12 Kt × B !, Kt—B3; 13 P—K4 !, Kt—QR4; 14 Kt—K3.

12 . . . .   Q—Kt2 ch !
13 K—Kt1 ?

Lifeless. Better was 13 Kt—B3 (not 13 P—B3 ? ?, P—KKt4; 14 Q—Q2, P—KR3 !).

13	Q—R3
14 Q—Kt3	Kt—B3

15 KR—Q1

He has no choice, for if 15 Kt—B3 (too late, but 15 P × P, KtP × P followed by . . . QR—Kt1 is even worse for him), Kt—QR4; 16 Q—Kt5, Q × Q; 17 P × Q, Kt—B5; 18 B—B1, Kt—Q4 forcing the win of the Queen's Bishop Pawn.

15	Kt—QR4
16 Q—Kt5	Q × Q
17 P × Q	Kt—B5

The Knight is very powerful here—primarily because of the disappearance of White's white-squared Bishop. Black's game now "plays itself."

18 B—B1	P—QR3 !

Forcing open a new avenue of attack. White must soon crumple up.

19 KtP × P	R × P
20 P × P	KtP × P
21 Kt—Kt2	

Still wandering!

21	Kt—Q4

Black's Knights are magnificent.

22 R—Q3	KR—R1
23 P—K4	Kt—K4 !

White resigns, as he realizes the hopelessness of 24 R—Q1, Kt × P; 25 R—B1, R × P; 26 R × R, Kt—B6 *ch !;* 27 K—R1, R × R and the King's Pawn goes.

[181

49. Fuzzy-Wuzzy

THERE are some players, and Bogolyubov is outstanding among them, who must attack at all times in all positions. Their desire to attack is not always grounded on rational considerations; this often leads to crises which demand a ruthless decision to renounce the attack. But renunciation is hard, and they hate to cope with reality. They would do well to remember the old jingle:

> Fuzzy Wuzzy was a bear,
> Fuzzy Wuzzy lost his hair.
> Then Fuzzy Wuzzy wasn't fuzzy,
> Was he?

NIMZOINDIAN DEFENSE

San Remo, 1930

WHITE: *E. Bogolyubov*   BLACK: *A. Nimzovich*

1 P—Q4	Kt—KB3
2 P—QB4	P—K3
3 Kt—QB3	B—Kt5
4 Q—Kt3	

In the late '30s this was to be replaced in popular favor by the more sedate 4 Q—B2; later on, the even quieter alternative 4 P—K3 was to become fashionable.

4	P—B4

4 . . . Kt—B3 is a promis-

ing alternative, leading to a complicated game.

5 P × P	Kt—B3
6 Kt—B3	Kt—K5
7 B—Q2	Kt × QBP
8 Q—B2	P—B4

Customary but not essential. In a famous game against Stahlberg at Hamburg later in the same year, Kashdan demonstrated that after 8 . . . O—O; 9 P—K4 ?, Q—B3 ! etc. Black has a very strong game.

9 P—K3

9 P—QR3 is doubtless best here, for example 9 . . . B × Kt; 10 B × B, O—O; 11 P—QKt4, Kt—K5; 12 B—Kt2 and White has a promising game because of his two Bishops and pressure on the Queen file.

9	O—O
10 B—K2	P—QKt3
11 O—O—O	

After castling King-side, White would be exposed to a strong attack by . . . B—Kt2 in combination with . . . R—B3—Kt3. After the text, White's King is also insecure.

Bogolyubov looks forward to a technically simple and amply rewarding action against Black's backward Queen's

Pawn. Hence Nimzovich loses no time in taking counter-measures.

11 . . . .   P—QR4 !

Beginning an attack whose subtlety is quite lost on his opponent.

12 P—QR3   P—R5 ! !

Who but Nimzovich would have devised this inspired method of avoiding the exchange of the Bishop for the Knight?! If now 13 P × B ?, Kt × P; 14 Q—Kt1, Kt—Kt6 mate !

13 Kt—QKt5	B × B ch
14 Kt × B	Kt—R4
15 B—B3	P—Q4 !
16 P × P	B—R3 !

Virtually leaving White without a move, for if 17 B—K2 (17 Kt—B3, B—Q6 wins the Queen, or if 17 Kt—Q4, R—B1; 18 Kt—B6, R × Kt; 19 P × R, B—Q6), R—B1; 18 K—Kt1, Kt(B4)—Kt6; 19 Q—Q3, R—B4 and wins.

17 Kt—B4 ! ?	B × Kt
18 P × P	

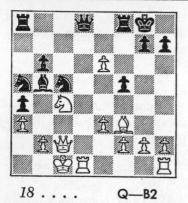

18 . . . .   Q—B2

Even more conclusive, says Nimzovich, was 18 . . . B × Kt *!;* 19 R × Q, QR × Q; 20 R —Q1 (not 20 P—K7, Kt(R4) —Kt6 *ch;* 21 K—Kt1, B—Q6 winning White's Queen), B × P etc.

19 B × R	B × Kt
20 B—Q5	B × B
21 R × B	Q—B3
22 P—K7	Q × R
23 P × R(Q) *ch*	K × Q
24 R—Q1	Q—K4

The situation has cleared: Black has two Knights against Rook and Pawn and should win, albeit with some difficulty.

25 P—R3	P—R4
26 P—KKt4 *?*	

But this "attacking" move hastens the end by further weakening the white squares. The following play, in which Nimzovich cleverly combines centralized maneuvers of his Queen with powerful support by the Knights, is worthy of close study.

26	RP × P
27 P × P	Kt(R4)— Kt6 *ch !*
28 K—Kt1	P × P

Nimzovich has provided for 29 Q—R7, which he will answer with 29 . . . Q—K5 *ch;* 30 Q × Q, Kt × Q; 31 R— Kt1, Kt × P; 32 R—Kt2, Kt— Q7 *ch;* 33 K—B2, Kt(Q7)— K5; 34 P—Kt3, P—QKt4 and White's King is powerless to approach the scene of action!

29 R—Kt1   Q—Q4
30 R—Q1

And not 30 R × P *P P*, Q—R8 *ch* followed by mate.

30 . . . .   Q—K5
31 R—Kt1

Exchanging Queens loses the Bishop's Pawn.

31 . . . .   Kt—Q7 *ch*
32 K—B1   Q—Q4 *!*

Forcing a quick win, as 33 P—Kt4, Kt(4)—Kt6 *ch;* 34 K—Kt2, Kt—B5 *ch;* 35 K—R2, Kt—Q5; 36 Q × P, P—QKt4;

37 Q—R7, Kt—R4 *ch* leads to mate (Nimzovich).

33 Q—R7   Kt(7)—K5
34 Q—R8 *ch*   K—B2
35 K—Kt1

Amusing is 35 R—Q1, Kt—Kt6 *ch;* 36 K—B2, Q—B5 *ch;* 37 K—Kt1, Kt(5)—Q7 *ch* and mate in two.

35 . . . .   Q—Q6 *ch*

White resigns, for if 36 K—R2 (36 K—R1, Kt—Kt6 *ch* produces the same position), Kt—B6 *ch* leads to mate.

50. *Success or Failure?*

ELMER DAVIS gave an old bromide a new twist when he wrote that "Nothing fails like success." What he had in mind, no doubt, was that thoughtless aping of a great man's successes will often lead to sorry failures.

In this game, the only rational idea that Ahues has is to establish the Queen-side majority of Pawns. Does this advantage win by force? Ahues seems to think so. But his powerful opponent's forceful, logical and original play puts the matter in a different light. The most absorbing feature of this fine game is the brilliant success scored by Nimzovich in reducing the Queen-side majority to impotence.

This must have given him particular pleasure, for there was nothing which delighted the Hypermoderns more than to upset one of the all-too-hackneyed postulates dear to followers of the classical theories. Once modern, they have now become musty. One day the wheel will turn again.

CARO-KANN DEFENSE

San Remo, 1930

WHITE: *K. Ahues*   BLACK: *A. Nimzovich*

1	P—K4	P—QB3
2	P—Q4	P—Q4
3	Kt—QB3	P × P
4	Kt × P	Kt—B3

Regarding this move, see Game 56.

5	Kt—Kt3	P—B4
6	Kt—B3	P × P

It may well be that 6 . . . Kt—B3 gives more practical chances. The text leads to an ending in which White's Queen-side majority of Pawns, his superior development and the preferable placement of his pieces assure him better prospects.

7	Q × P	Q × Q
8	Kt × Q	P—QR3

Else Kt—Kt5 can be unpleasant.

9	B—K2	P—KKt3

In a later game at Frankfort the same year against Thomas, Nimzovich played to get rid of White's formidable King's Bishop: 9 . . . B—Kt5; 10 B—Q3, P—K4; 11 Kt(4)—B5, P—KKt3; 12 Kt—K3, QKt—Q2; 13 Kt—K4. Black's game was far from easy to play.

10	O—O	B—Kt2

White's position is highly satisfactory. He should now play 11 B—B3, leaving Black

nothing better than 11 . . .
Kt—Kt5; 12 P—B3, Kt—K4;
13 B—Q5 and Black will have
to weaken his Pawn position in
order to drive off the annoying
Bishop.

11 R—Q1   O—O
12 P—QB3

B—B3 was still the move.

12 . . . .   B—Kt5 !

Forcing the removal of the
dangerous Bishop, as 13 P—
B3 is too weakening and 13 Kt
—B3 allows . . . Kt—B3.

13 B—K3   B × B
14 Kt(4) × B

He should recapture with
the other Knight, which is de-
centralized.

14 . . . .   R—B1 !

This and the next few moves
are dedicated to the important
positional task of paralyzing
White's Queen-side majority.

15 R—Q2   Kt—B3
16 QR—Q1   Kt—K4

Now White must prevent
. . . Kt—B5.

17 P—Kt3   P—QKt4 !
18 P—KR3   P—K3 !

With P—QB4 prevented,
Nimzovich supports the posting of a Knight at Q4.

19 P—KB4   Kt—B3
20 K—B2   P—KR4

Threatening . . . P—R5
followed by . . . Kt—K5 ch.
But the deeper significance of
the move is that Nimzovich
means to occupy K5 perma-
nently. Note that the white
squares in White's camp are
weak (Q3,K4) and that his
pieces have little scope.

21 R—Q3   P—R5
22 Kt—KB1   Kt—K2
23 B—Q4   Kt—K5 ch !
24 K—K3   B × B ch !

[187

If now 25 R × B (25 K ×
B?, Kt—B7), Kt × P wins a
Pawn, while 25 P × B leads to
an isolated Queen's Pawn with
a fatal weakening of White's
game. There remains only:

25 K × Kt   B—Kt3 *!*

He changes to a better diagonal.

26 Kt—K3   K—B1
27 R(1)—Q2   K—K1
28 R—Q1   R—B2
29 R—QR1   Kt—B3

Nimzovich plans to react
powerfully in the center against
White's contemplated diversion on the Queen-side.

30 P—R4   P—B4 *ch*
31 K—B3   P—K4 *!*
32 R—Q6   P—K5 *ch*
33 K—B2   R—Q1 *!*

Having suddenly secured a
formidable passed Pawn, Nimzovich realizes that removal of
the Rooks will enhance its
strength.

34 R × R *ch*

If 34 R × P??, R—Q6 and
White can resign. An interesting possibility pointed out by

188]

Kostich is 34 R(1)—Q1, K—
K2 *!;* 35 R × R, Kt × R; 36 Kt
—Q4, R—Q2 *!;* 37 Kt(3)—
B2, Kt—B3; 38 K—K3, P—
Kt5 *!;* 39 P × P, Kt × Kt; 40
Kt × Kt, R × Kt; 41 R × R, K
—B2 and White's Rook ex-
pires in *Zugzwang!*

34 . . . .   K × R
35 P × P   P × P
36 R—Q1 *ch*
'

The pin is very troublesome
for White. If however 36 R—
R6, B—R2 followed by . . .
K—B1—Kt2 and . . . R—Q2
winning easily.

36 . . . .   R—Q2
37 R × R *ch*   K × R

The exchanges have left
Black with an interesting winning method.

White is lost, as the following fascinating variations prove: 38 P—Kt3, Kt—K2 and now:

I 39 P × P, Kt—Q4; 40 Kt —Q4, Kt × Kt; 41 K × Kt, P —Kt5; 42 K—Q2, P × P *ch;* 43 K × P, B × Kt *ch;* 44 K × B, K—Q3 and the ending is lost for White!

II 39 P—B4, P × P *ch;* 40 Kt × P, P—Kt4 *!;* 41 Kt—R5, Kt—Kt3 *!;* 42 K—K2, KKtP × P; 43 Kt(3) × P, P × P; 44

P × P, K—K3 with an easy win.

38	P—QKt4	K—K3
39	Kt—B1	P—Kt4
40	Kt—K2	K—B3

White has run into *Zugzwang* and a Pawn must fall.

41	Kt—Q4	B × Kt

41 . . . Kt × Kt allows 42 Kt—Q5 *ch.* After the text, White can resign.

42	P × P *ch*	K × P
43	P × B	Kt × KtP *!*
44	K—K2	P—B5
45	Kt—Q1	Kt—Q4
46	K—Q2	K—B4
47	Kt—Kt2	Kt—K6

White resigns. A beautiful example of powerfully centralized play. Apparently Ahues was greatly mystified!

51. The Isolated Queen's Pawn

READERS who are familiar with the famous chapter in *My System* which deals with the isolated Queen's Pawn and "his descendants" will find an absorbing illustration of the theme in this game. White uses the Pawn as an attacking instrument (support of the aggressive outpost K5); Black tries to make similar use of the pivot point Q4 (with a view to simplifying exchanges). But Nimzovich's brilliantly conceived attack strikes home first—and with what deadly rapidity!

CARO-KANN DEFENSE

Copenhagen, 1930

(Simultaneous Exhibition)

WHITE: *A. Nimzovich*   BLACK: *W. Nielsen*

1	P—K4	P—QB3
2	P—Q4	P—Q4
3	Kt—QB3	P × P
4	Kt × P	Kt—Q2
5	Kt—KB3	KKt—B3

If now 6 Kt × Kt *ch,* Kt × Kt and Black has an easy game, as he gets his Queen's Bishop to B4 or Kt5.

6	Kt—Kt3	P—K3
7	B—Q3	P—B4 *!*

A necessary freeing move.

8	O—O	B—K2
9	P—B3	

Indicating that he is willing to accept the responsibility of the isolated Queen's Pawn. An easier alternative is 9 R—K1, P—QKt3; 10 P—B4, P × P; 11 Kt × P, B—Kt2 (Spielmann—Hönlinger, 1929) and now 12 Kt(3)—B5 *!* with a good attack.

White's chief reason for being willing to accept an iso-

| 13 | Q × B | P × P |
| 14 | P × P | Kt—Q4 |

Black has given his opponent the isolated Pawn and occupies the pivot point in the approved theoretical fashion. But Nimzovich will teach him a few fine points.

| 15 | B—K4 ! | QKt—B3 |
| 16 | B—K5 | |

The Bishop is ideally centralized, aiming at the hostile King-side and guarding the Queen's Pawn at the same time.

| 16 | . . . . | Kt × B |
| 17 | Kt × Kt | Kt—B3 |

Has he read *My System*?! He plays for simplification (the strongest weapon against the isolated Pawn), but in this case the rule leads him astray. Better was 17 . . . R—B1, although in that case White keeps the initiative with 18 Q —KKt3.

18 QR—B1 !

Placing the Rook on the open file and heading for the seventh rank. Note that Black

lated Queen's Pawn is that Black's pieces will be unable to get to QB4 or K4.

9	. . . .	O—O
10	R—K1	P—QKt3
11	P—KR3	

At this stage, the advance of the Pawn serves no conceivable purpose. Yet it ultimately validates the soundness of White's crucial combination!

| 11 | . . . . | B—Kt2 |
| 12 | B—KB4 | B × Kt |

He is too eager to give his opponent the isolated Queen's Pawn. Quite promising was the alternative 12 . . . Kt—Q4; 13 B—Q2, Q—B2 and the prospect of . . . Kt—B5 can be very annoying for White.

cannot parry with 18 . . . R —B1; for then 19 R × R, Q × R; 20 Kt × Kt *ch* wins a Pawn and rips up his King's position irremediably.

18	Kt × Kt
19 R × Kt	

The Rook reports for the attack. Black should now defend with 19 . . . B—Q3 to prevent R—B7; but he is still bemused by routine positional ideas.

19	Q—Q4
20 R—B7 !	

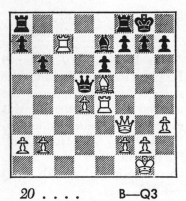

20	B—Q3

This allows Nimzovich to wind up brilliantly, but there was no longer any fool-proof defense, for example:

I   20 . . . B—Q1; 21 R —Kt4, P—Kt3; 22 Q × Q, P × Q; 23 R—Q7 winning a Pawn with an easily won ending.

II   20 . . . KR—K1; 21 B × P *!*, K × B (or 21 . . . P— B4; 22 Q—KKt3 *!* and Black is helpless); 22 R—Kt4 *ch*, K —B1; 23 Q—KKt3 *!* and wins.

21 R—Q7	QR—Q1
22 R × B !	R × R
23 Q—B6 ! !	

Black *resigns!* If 23 . . . P × Q; 24 R—Kt4 *ch* and mate next move; or 23 . . . Q × B; 24 Q × Q.

Note that if White's Pawn had been left on KR2, Black could have extricated himself with 20 . . . QR—B1 *!*

52. *Fish*

IT IS curious that chessplayers are divided so sharply into categories. The man who is a big fish in a little pond will often turn out to be only a minnow in a bigger pond. The city or county champion plays like Superman in his bailiwick: he is brilliant, resourceful, unbeatable. Put him in the state championship, and he becomes a bumble-fingered tail-ender.

So it is with Ahues. One would never guess from the way Nimzovich batters him that in less exalted company Ahues is a sly and able tactician. What it all adds up to, of course, is indirect praise of Nimzovich: these two players were not in the same class.

NIMZOVICH ATTACK

Frankfort, 1930

WHITE: *A. Nimzovich*   BLACK: *K. Ahues*

1 Kt—KB3	P—Q4
2 P—QKt3	P—K3
3 B—Kt2	Kt—KB3
4 P—K3	QKt—Q2
5 P—B4	P—B3

Too conservative; since he later loses time with a second move with this Pawn, he should have played . . . B—Q3 at once, deferring the advance of the Queen's Bishop Pawn to a later stage.

6 Kt—B3	B—Q3

In effect, Black is playing the Colle System with colors reversed. Such opening setups have to be handled in a judicious manner.

7 Q—B2	Q—K2

Had he played 7 . . . P—K4 there would have followed 8 P × P, P × P (if 8 . . . Kt × P; 9 Kt—K4, B—B2; 10 B

[193

—R3); 9 Kt—QKt5, B—Kt1;
10 B—R3 etc. The following
play revolves about Black's attempts to free himself by advancing in the center.

8 Kt—Q4

A sure way to restrain . . .
P—K4, but it allows 8 . . . P
—B4 (gaining a tempo for
Black). Then 9 KKt—Kt5, B—
Kt1 leaves the Knight poorly
situated; it has to retreat to B3.

8 . . . .   P—QR3

As the game goes, and as the
previous note indicates, this
move is waste of time.

9 B—K2   O—O
10 O—O   P—B4
11 Kt—B3   Kt—Kt3 ?

Black insists on asserting
himself in the center. The text
is played to prepare for . . .
P—K4, but it has the very
serious drawback of removing
the Knight from the center—
the vital theater of action.

Simple and good was 11
. . . P—QKt3 followed by 12
. . . B—Kt2.

12 P—K4 !

Beginning a sharp skirmish
in the course of which he will
exploit the absence of Black's
Queen Knight from the center.

12 . . . .   Kt × KP

There is little choice, as 12
. . . P—Q5; 13 P—K5, P ×
Kt; 14 P × B, Q × P; 15 Q ×
P is very much in White's
favor. The absence of Black's
Knight is already beginning to
be felt!

13 Kt × Kt   P × Kt
14 Q × P   P—K4 ?

Ahues has deliberately
aimed for this position. The
King's Pawn cannot be cap-
tured (15 B × P ?, B × B; 16
Q × B, Q × Q; 17 Kt × Q, R
—K1; 18 P—B4, P—B3 and

wins) and Black is ready to play . . . P—B4 with a fine game. But Nimzovich has his own ideas.

15 Kt × P *!!*   R—K1

The main line of Nimzovich's calculations was 15 . . . P—B3 (not 15 . . . B × Kt; 16 Q × B, Q × Q; 17 B × Q, R—K1; 18 B—B7 with a Pawn ahead); 16 B—Q3, P × Kt (obviously, if 16 . . . P—Kt3; 17 Kt—B3 with a Pawn to the good; if 16 . . . B × Kt; 17 Q × P *ch*, K—B2; 18 QR—K1 followed by 19 P—B4 with a winning attack); 17 Q × P *ch*, K—B2; 18 Q—Kt6 *ch*, K—Kt1; 19 P—B4 and Black is helpless.

16 P—B4   P—B3
17 B—R5 *!*

A daring but quite sound idea: the presence of the Black Rook on K1 leads to a variety of ingenious attacking motifs.

17 . . . .   R—B1

Nimzovich refutes the alternatives as follows:

I 17 . . . R—Q1; 18 B—B7 *ch*, K—R1; 19 Kt—Kt6 *ch*, P × Kt; 20 Q × KKtP, B—Kt5; 21 QR—K1 with the irresistible threat R—K3—R3 *ch* followed by Q—R5 mate.

II 17 . . . P—Kt3; 18 B × P, P × B; 19 Q × P *ch*, K—B1; 20 Kt—Kt4 *!*, B × Kt; 21 B × P and Black is helpless.

18 P—Q3 *!*   P × Kt

Realizing that after 18 . . . P—Kt3; 19 B × P White has too many Pawns and too much

[195

play for the piece, Ahues decides to make a quick end of it.

19 P × P   B—B2

Black's pieces have no scope,
but if 19 . . . P—Kt3; 20 R ×
R *ch* followed by 21 B × P
wins rapidly.

20 R × R *ch*   Q × R
21 R—KB1   Q—Q1

On 21 . . . Q—K2; 22 R
—B7 wins easily.

22 B—B7 *ch*   K—R1
23 P—K6   B × P

If he tries to prevent P—K7
by playing 23 . . . Q—K2,
then 24 B × P *ch !*, K × B; 25
Q—Kt4 *ch*, K—R3; 26 R—B5
followed by mate. Again poor
Ahues has been outgeneraled!

24 B × B   Q—Kt4
25 R—B7   Resigns

Black's pieces never budged.

53. *Planning Beats Guessing*

I N THIS game, both players resort to clever tactical devices.
The difference in their approach is that Mannheimer im-
provises little threats which only *temporize;* Nimzovich's
tactical finesses, however, mesh into a broadly conceived
strategical plan. The result is that Mannheimer must eventually file a petition in bankruptcy.

FRENCH DEFENSE

Frankfort, 1930

WHITE: *Dr. N. Mannheimer*   BLACK: *A. Nimzovich*

1 P—K4   P—K3
2 P—Q4   P—Q4
3 Kt—QB3   B—Kt5
4 P × P

Now Black has an easy
game. 4 P—K5 is the move.

4 . . . .   P × P
5 Kt—B3

5 B—Q3 followed by 6 Kt—K2 is preferable.

5 . . . .   Kt—K2
6 B—Q3   QKt—B3
7 P—KR3

Else . . . B—Kt5 might be annoying.

7 . . . .   B—KB4
8 B × B   Kt × B

Now White cannot avoid some deterioration of his Pawn position. Thus if 9 Q—Q3, Q—K2 *ch;* 10 B—K3, Kt × B; 11 P × Kt, O—O—O and White is left with a weak King's Pawn.

9 O—O   B × Kt
10 P × B   O—O

Nimzovich's plan is clear: mastery of the white squares based on the absence of White's King Bishop. White is to be restrained from advancing P—B4 and dissolving his doubled Pawn. Occupation of K5 and QB5 by the Black Knights is already indicated.

11 Q—Q3   Kt—Q3

Despite his positional disadvantage, White has chances.

12 Kt—Kt5

Despite its superficial appearance, this move is part of a strategically valuable plan: White wants to create counterbalancing strength on the black squares.

12 . . . .   P—KKt3
13 B—B4   Q—B3 !

The effort to save one of the precious Knights would not do at all: 13 . . . Kt—B5 ?; 14 Q—Kt3, R—B1; 15 Q—R4 with a winning position.

14 B—Q2

He has the courage of his convictions: 14 B × Kt was the safe move.

14 . . . .   P—KR3 !
15 Kt—B3   K—R2

[197

16 Kt—R2

Threatening Kt—Kt4. If
now 16 . . . Q—Kt2; 17 Kt
—Kt4, P—KR4; 18 B—R6
winning the exchange.

16 . . . .   Q—R1 *!*

One of those extraordinary
moves for which Nimzovich
was famous. The position of
the Queen deserves a diagram.

17 Q—K3   Q—Kt2 *!*
18 Q—B3

If instead 18 Kt—Kt4, P—
B4 *!;* 19 Q × P *ch* ? (or 19 Kt
× P ?, Kt—B5), Q × Q; 20 Kt
× Q (if 20 B × Q, R—R1
wins a piece), Kt—K5; 21 B—
B1, P—KKt4; 22 P—B3, Kt—
Kt6; 23 B × P, Kt × R; 24 K
× Kt, K—Kt3; 25 P—KR4, R

—R1 with an easy win. White
will soon be encircled.

18 . . . .   Kt—K5
19 B—B1   P—B4
20 Q—Q3   Kt—R4

The initiative has obviously
passed to Black, and Nimzovich begins the play on the
white squares with his customary skill in such matters.

21 P—KB4 *!*

Rightly playing to establish
his Knight on the strong point
K5. 21 Q—Kt5, P—Kt3; 22
Q × QP, Kt × QBP is good
for Black.

21 . . . .   Q—Q2
22 Kt—B3   Q—B3
23 Kt—K5   Q—K3

But not 23 . . . Q × P ?;
24 Q × Q, Kt × Q; 25 B—Q2,
Kt—K7 *ch;* 26 K—B2 winning
a piece.

24 R—Kt1   P—Kt3
25 K—R2   Kt—B5
26 B—K3

He leaves the Black Knights
in their dominating position;
for if 26 Kt × Kt, P × Kt; 27

Q—K3, Q—Q4 the Bishop is crippled, and sooner or later Black will break through with . . . P—B4 and . . . P—KKt4.

26 . . . .   P—KKt4 !

As in so many modern games, we see Black operating on both wings. He establishes powerful pressure on the Kingside in order to . . . win on the other flank!

27 P—Kt3   R—B3
28 QR—K1   R—KKt1
29 B—B1   P—Kt4 !

Clearing the path to QR3.

30 Kt—B3 ?

This hastens the end, by allowing Black to force the immediate opening of the King Knight file.

30 . . . .   P—KKt5
31 P × P   R × P
32 Kt—Kt1   R(3)—Kt3

But not 32 . . . R × KtP ?; 33 R × Kt ! and wins.

33 R—B3   Q—Kt1

The King Knight Pawn was still immune. Note that Nimzovich is in no hurry to go after the doomed Queen Rook Pawn.

34 Kt—K2   P—KR4
35 K—Kt2   P—R5

Who would believe that this wing is not the side on which Black will achieve victory?

36 R—R1   R—R3
37 R—R3   Q—Kt3 ! !

Black plans an exquisite *Zugzwang* position: 38 . . . P × P; 39 R × R *ch* (39 Kt × P leads to the same line), Q × R; 40 Kt × P, Q—R5; 41 P—R3, P—R4 and any move by White loses!

38 B—K3   Q—R3 !

Another masterly move.

Black actually threatens to win the hostile Queen (! !) with 39 . . . Kt—Kt7 !

| 39 B—B2 | Q × P |
| 40 B—K1 | P—R4 ! |

The finish is hilarious: because White's pieces are tied to the defense of the King-side, he must permit the following promenade of the Rook's Pawn:

41 K—B1	Q—Kt8
42 Kt—Kt1	P—R5
43 K—K2	P—R6
44 R—B1	P—R7

White resigns. This is one of the great masterpieces of blockading strategy.

54.   No Retreat?

IN CHESS, there is a time to attack and a time to defend; a time to force the issue, and a time to consolidate one's position; a time to advance, and a time to retreat. Rudolf Spielmann was one of the most brilliant attacking players of all time, but discretion was not one of his virtues. He would not have cared for Wellington's definition of greatness in a general: "To know when to retreat and to *dare* to do it." But that counsel would not have been wasted on Nimzovich, who applied it in many an arduous game.

CARO-KANN DEFENSE

Bled, 1931

WHITE: *R. Spielmann*   BLACK: *A. Nimzovich*

1 P—K4	P—QB3
2 Kt—KB3	P—Q4
3 Kt—B3	P × P
4 Kt × P	Kt—B3

5 Kt—Kt3

As explained in the notes to Game 56, Kt × Kt *ch* is the most promising move.

5 . . . .   P—B4

Inviting White to simplify by 6 P—Q4, P × P; 7 Q × P, Q × Q; 8 Kt × Q etc. But Spielmann naturally prefers complications. His problem in the play that follows is to create winning possibilities without unduly compromising his position. His cunning opponent is fully aware of the dilemma.

6 B—B4   P—QR3
7 P—QR4   Kt—B3
8 P—Q3

One of the consequences of Spielmann's treatment of the opening is that he must be content with a more modest position in the center than is usually White's lot in this opening.

8 . . . .   P—KKt3
9 B—K3   B—Kt2
10 O—O

Threatening 11 B × BP (if 10 B × BP, Q—R4 *ch* with advantage).

10 . . . .   P—Kt3

The coming play will revolve about Spielmann's attempt to weaken Black's game by forcing P—R5. Nimzovich will be resourceful in countermeasures.

11 P—B3   O—O
12 P—R3   B—Kt2
13 Q—K2   Kt—QR4
14 B—R2   B—Q4

Nimzovich pursues his favorite theme of centralization, although 14 . . . Kt—Q4 is equally good.

15 Kt—Q2 !

Still angling for the eventual P—R5.

15 . . . .   B × B
16 R × B   Kt—Q4
17 Kt—B4   Kt—QB3

He deems 17 . . . Kt × Kt; 18 P × Kt, Kt × B; 19 Q

[201

× Kt, P—QR4 too simplify-
ing.

18 P—R5   P—QKt4
19 Kt—Kt6 !

Spielmann has achieved his
object and now sacrifices a
Pawn temporarily.

19 . . . .   Kt × Kt
20 P × Kt   Q × KtP
21 Kt—K4   Q—B2
22 Kt × P   P—QR4
23 P—Q4   KR—Kt1

Both players have obtained
pretty much what they wanted.
White has rid himself of his
weak Queen Rook Pawn and
advanced his Queen's Pawn;
Black has the minority attack
on the Queen-side, giving him
a slight initiative.

24 P—KB4 ?

This loosens up White's position without giving him gen-
uine attacking chances. Either
24 Q—B3 or 24 R—Q1 suf-
fices to maintain the balance
of power.

24 . . . .   P—K3 !

Prevents P—B5 and pre-
pares . . . Kt—K2—Q4 with
powerful centralization.

25 R(2)—R1   Kt—K2
26 P—KKt4 ?

Consistent but bad. The intended advance of the King's
Bishop Pawn is doomed to failure.

26 . . . .   Kt—Q4
27 R—B3

If 27 P—B5 ? ?, Q—Kt6 ch.

27 . . . .   P—R5
28 B—Q2   Q—B3
29 Kt—K4

29 Q—Q1 offers a some-
what better defense.

29 . . . .   P—Kt5 !
30 P—B5

At last comes the move on which Spielmann has spent so much eager preparation; but now his position is demolished by Nimzovich's sharp and clear play.

30	. . . .	KP × P *!*
31	KtP × P	P—R6 *!*
32	KtP × P	P × QBP *!*

A classic example of demolition strategy. If now 33 B × P, Kt × B is murder.

| 33 | P—B6 | P × B *!* |
| 34 | P × B | R—K1 *!* |

Black's advanced passed Pawn is destined to live a charmed life. The immediate threat is . . . P—B4.

| 35 | Q—Q3 | R × Kt *!* |
| 36 | Q × R | R—K1 |

Now White is punished for having opened up his game so optimistically. If he tries 37 Q —Q3 there follows 37 . . . R —K8 *ch;* 38 R—B1, Q—B8; 39 R—Kt1, Kt—K6 and wins.

| 37 | Q—R4 | Kt—B6 |
| 38 | R(3)—B1 | Q—Q4 *!* |

White *resigns,* for if 39 P— R4, R—K5; 40 Q—B2, R— K7; 41 Q—B3, Q × Q; 42 R × Q, R—K8 *ch;* 43 R—B1, R × R; 44 R × R, Kt—K7 *ch;* 45 K—B2, Kt—B8 *!* and wins.

55. Sorcerer's Apprentice

IN SUCH encounters as Game 4 we saw how Nimzovich, as a promising master in his twenties, gained international recognition by victories against the famous, established masters of his day.

In the present game, we see the middle-aged Nimzovich playing against the younger masters of more modern times. At this stage, Nimzovich was beginning to have trouble holding his own against the youngsters who had been brought up on his theories and were applying his ideas in their own games.

Yet we can sense here that Flohr is overwhelmed at the thought of playing against the man from whom he has learned so much. Flohr's timidity soon condemns him to a cramped position, which Nimzovich exploits with all his proverbial skill in such situations.

OLD-INDIAN DEFENSE

(in effect)

Bled, 1931

WHITE: *A. Nimzovich*   BLACK: *S. Flohr*

1 P—QB4	Kt—KB3
2 Kt—QB3	P—K3
3 P—K4	P—Q3 ?

An unnecessarily conservative move which crowds Black's pieces badly. The approved equalizing line is 3 . . . P—Q4; 4 P—K5, P—Q5!

| 4 P—Q4 | P—K4 |

Black has lost a tempo to play an inferior variation!

| 5 KKt—K2 | B—K2 |

Somewhat more promising is 5 . . . P—KKt3 followed by 6 . . . B—Kt2.

6 P—B3	P—B3

Black must adopt the Hanham System to get some scope for his pieces, but even at this early stage of the game, it has already become questionable whether he can overcome the disadvantage of his inferior opening.

7 B—K3	Q—B2
8 Q—Q2	QKt—Q2
9 P—Q5 !	Kt—Kt3

On 9 . . . O—O there follows 10 P—KKt4 and 11 Kt —Kt3 with a powerful attacking position for White.

10 Kt—Kt3	B—Q2

An important finesse: if 10 . . . P × P; 11 BP × P, Kt—B5 ?; 12 Kt—Kt5 ! and wins.

11 P—Kt3 !

Nimzovich has played the opening with fine judgment and his position makes a very favorable impression. Flohr has so little confidence in his position that he now undertakes a demonstration which only hastens the end.

11	P—KR4
12 B—Q3	P—Kt3
13 O—O	Kt—R2

Black has so many weaknesses on the King-side that he cannot very well castle on that wing.

14 P—QR4 !

Threatening to cramp his opponent's game still further by the advance of this Pawn.

14	P—R5
15 KKt—K2	P—QB4
16 P—B4 !	

The indicated move. In order to neutralize the pressure on the King Bishop file, Black will be forced to create new weaknesses.

16	P × P
17 R × P	

[205

17 . . . .   P—Kt4

The exchange of Bishops would not help: 17 . . . B—KKt4; 18 R—B2, B × B; 19 Q × B, P—Kt4; 20 QR—KB1, P—B3; 21 P—K5 ! !, QP × P; 22 B—Kt6 *ch*, K—Q1; 23 Kt—K4, QR—B1; 24 Kt × KBP, Kt × Kt; 25 Q × KtP and wins.

Black can hardly avoid a brilliant demolition.

18 R—B2   P—B3

Black seems to have consolidated his position and is now ready for . . . Kt—KB1—Kt3—K4.

19 P—K5 ! !

A well-timed thrust which opens new attacking lines for White's pieces. If now 19 . . .

BP × P; 20 B—Kt6 *ch*, K—Q1; 21 R—B7, Kt—KB1; 22 R × B !, Kt × B; 23 Kt—Kt5 !, Q—Kt1; 24 B × KtP !, Kt × R; 25 B × Kt *ch*, K × B forced; 26 Q—Kt5 *ch*, K—K1; 27 Q—Kt6 *ch* and wins.

19 . . . .   QP × P
20 B—Kt6 *ch*   K—Q1
21 Kt—K4 !

The point of the Pawn sacrifice. The threat of P—Q6 gives White sufficient time to strengthen the attack decisively.

21 . . . .   Kt—QB1
22 B × Kt   R × B
23 Kt × KBP   R—Kt2
24 B × KtP   Kt—Q3

A desperate hope which is elegantly refuted by Nimzovich.

25 B × P !   Kt—B4
26 R × Kt !

Neat simplification.

26 . . . .   B × R
27 P—Q6 !   Q × P
28 Q × Q *ch*   B × Q
29 Kt—R5 *ch*   R—K2
30 R—KB1

30 . . . .   B—Q6

On 30 . . . B—Kt3 or . . .
B—Q2 there follows 31 R—
B8 *ch*, B—K1; 32 Kt—Kt7,
K—Q2; 33 B × R, B × B; 34
R × B, R × R; 35 Kt × R, K ×
Kt; 36 Kt—B3 with an easy
endgame win.

31 R—B8 *ch*   K—Q2

Or 31 . . . K—B2; 32 R ×
R, R—R2; 33 B—Q8 *ch !*, K
—B3; 34 Kt—B6 ! with R—
B8 *ch* to follow.

32 R × R   B × Kt
33 B × R

All this has been beautifully
calculated by Nimzovich.

33 . . . .   B × B
34 Kt—Kt3   B—Q8
35 Kt—B5   B—Q1

It is clear that Black cannot
stop for 35 . . . P—R3 because of 36 Kt × B, K × Kt; 37
R—QKt8.

36 R × P   K—B3
37 R—R8   K—Q2
38 Kt—K3   B × P
39 K—B2   P—K5
40 R × B *ch !*   K × R
41 P—R5   B—R7
42 P—Kt4   Resigns

Nimzovich has played the
whole game in his best style.
Flohr never overcame the ef-
fects of his bad opening play.

56.   *"No Such Animal"*

TEMPERAMENT plays a potent if often unrealized role
in master chess. The average player is timid in the face
of promising attacking opportunities against a celebrated
master. He cannot believe the evidence of his senses: he is

[207

playing not only the master, but the master's reputation as well. The average player is like the rustic who, on beholding a giraffe for the first time, commented incredulously: "There's no such animal."

CARO-KANN DEFENSE

Bled, 1931

WHITE: *Dr. L. Asztalos*   BLACK: *A. Nimzovich*

1 P—K4	P—QB3
2 P—Q4	P—Q4
3 Kt—QB3	P × P
4 Kt × P	Kt—B3
5 Kt × Kt *ch*	KP × Kt

Black cedes his opponent the familiar advantage of a Queen-side majority of Pawns and a generally freer game in order to assure himself of fighting chess—something he would not get after the safer and duller 4 . . . B—B4.

6 P—QB3	B—Q3
7 B—Q3	O—O
8 Q—B2 *!*	P—KR3

8 . . . P—KKt3 *?* can be very dangerous: 9 Kt—K2, Q—B2; 10 P—KR4, R—K1; 11 P—R5 with a winning attack (Znosko–Borovsky — Tartakover, Paris, 1925).

9 Kt—K2	Q—B2
10 B—K3	Kt—Q2
11 Q—Q2	R—K1

To guard against B × P.

12 Kt—Kt3

12 O—O—O *!* gives strong attacking chances.

12 . . . .   **B—B5 *! ?***

This smothers the attacking chances which might arise

from a more plausible continu-
ation like 12 . . . Kt—B1; 13
O—O, B—K3; 14 B × P, P ×
B; 15 Q × P (threatening 16
Kt—R5), B × Kt; 16 BP × B,
P—KB4; 17 B × P etc.

The move also has the additional merit of weakening
White's center; on the other
hand, White gets excellent
prospects from the opening of
the King's Bishop file.

20 P—Q5 ?

White misses a very good
opportunity at this point in 20
Kt—R5 ! (see the introductory
remarks), for example:

13	O—O	B × B
14	P × B	Kt—B1
15	R—B2	Q—K2
16	P—K4	B—K3
17	P—QR3	

Preparing to double Rooks.
Kt—B5 was also good.

I 20 . . . B—Kt5; 21 Kt ×
P *ch,* P × Kt; 22 P—R3 *!,* B—
K3; 23 Q × P, Q—B1; 24 Q—
R5 threatening 25 R × P fol-
lowed by P—K5.

| 17 | . . . . | P—QB4 |

Attacks the hostile center.

II 20 . . . QR—Q1; 21 P
—Q5, B—Kt5; 22 Kt × P *ch,*
P × Kt; 23 R × P, K—Kt2
(there is nothing better); 24 P
—K5 *! !*

18 QR—KB1

P—Q5 is not so good, as it
gives Black a very valuable
square at his K4.

| 18 | . . . . | P × P |
| 19 | P × P | Kt—Kt3 |

20	. . . .	B—Kt5
21	R—B1	QR—B1
22	KR—B1	Q—K4

In order to be able to play
. . . Q—B1 in reply to any
sacrificial lines.

Now the initiative changes
hands; the results of P—Q5
are already becoming apparent.

23 Q—KB2

Black threatened . . . Q—Q5 *ch* followed by . . . Kt—K4.

23 . . . .   P—R3
24 P—R3   B—Q2
25 KR—Q1

25 K—R2 was somewhat better.

25 . . . .   Q—Kt4
26 R × R   R × R
27 K—R2   Kt—K4
28 Kt—B5

This plausible move (threatening Kt—K7 *ch*) allows Nimzovich to force the game by a series of very ingenious moves.

28 . . . .   R—B8 *!*

29 R—Q2

There is nothing better, for if 29 B—B2 (29 R × R, Kt × B *!* or 29 B—K2, R × R transposing into the main line), R × R; 30 B × R, Kt—Q6 winning at least a Pawn, for if 31 Q—K2, B × Kt; 32 Q × Kt, Q—B5 *ch* etc.

29 . . . .   P—KKt3 *!*
30 Kt—K3

Or 30 Kt—Q4 (30 Kt—Kt3 *?*, Kt—Kt5 *ch !*), Kt × B; 31 R × Kt, Q—K4 *ch* winning a Pawn.

30 . . . .   B × P *!*

If now 31 K × B, R—R8 mate or 31 P × B, Kt—B6 *ch;* 32 Q × Kt, Q—Kt8 mate.

31 B—B1   B—Q2

Threatening . . . Q × Kt *!*

32 K—Kt1   B—Kt4

Renews the threat.

33 R—Q1   Q × Kt *!*
34 Q × Q   R × R
35 Q—Kt6   Kt—Kt5 *!*
36 P—Kt3   B × B

White resigns. A masterly recovery by Nimzovich.

57. Craftsmanship

SUCH adjectives as "masterly" and "superb" have been freely bestowed on this unobtrusively beautiful game. Sparkling combinations tell their own story and require no salesmanship; endings like this one, whose beauty lies in their logic, are often "born to blush unseen."

FRENCH DEFENSE

Zurich, 1934

WHITE: *Dr. E. Lasker*   BLACK: *A. Nimzovich*

1 P—K4	P—K3
2 P—Q4	P—Q4
3 Kt—QB3	B—Kt5
4 P—K5	P—QB4
5 B—Q2	

In later years, 5 P—QR3 was to become the fashionable move; but the reply 5 . . . B —R4 still requires clarifying.

5	Kt—K2
6 Kt—Kt5	B × B *ch*
7 Q × B	O—O
8 P—QB3	Kt—B4

A good alternative is 8 . . . QKt—B3; 9 Kt—B3, Q—Kt3 and Black stands well.

9 P—KKt4 ?

An unexpected move for a player of Lasker's strength; he weakens his Pawn position without compensation. Preferable was 9 B—Q3, B—Q2; 10 Kt—B3 (if 10 B × Kt, B × Kt *!*), P × P; 11 P × P, Q—Kt3 and while Black has an excellent game, White has not created any weaknesses.

9	Kt—R5
10 P—Kt5	

This also makes a bad impression, although the underlying idea is logical enough: he wants to allow . . . P—B3 only at the cost of opening the King Knight file for his Rooks.

The Tournament Book, however, recommends 10 O—O—

O, P—B3; 11 P—KB4 as more
natural and less weakening.

10	P × P
11 P × P	Kt—B3
12 O—O—O	Q—R4 !

Nimzovich's last move is a
very hard one to meet. If
White avoids the exchange of
Queens by 13 Kt—QB3, then
Black's attack will develop too
rapidly.

13 K—Kt1 ?

Relatively better was 13
Q × Q, keeping his King near
the center and getting a normal development, thus: 13
. . . Kt × Q; 14 P—B4 !, P—
B3; 15 KtP × P, P × P; 16 Kt
—K2 and White is much better off than in the text continuation.

| 13 . . . . | Q × Q |
| 14 R × Q | P—B3 ! |

Probing into White's weaknesses: 15 P—B4 ? is impossible because of 15 . . . P ×
KtP etc.

| 15 KtP × P | P × P |

Now White still cannot play
the normal P—B4.

16 B—R3	P × P
17 Kt—B7	R—Kt1
18 Kt × KP	R—B3
19 Kt—B7	B × B
20 Kt × B	Kt—B6

White has completed his development, but the position of
his forces is still very awkward.

21 QR—Q1	P × P
22 Kt × P	R—B4
23 Kt(5)—B4	QR—KB1

White is hard pressed. It requires all of Lasker's skill to
hold the position together.

| 24 Kt—Q3 | Kt(3)—K4 |
| 25 Kt × Kt | R × Kt |
| 26 Kt—Kt1 ! ? |

This leads to a sharp skirmish. Lasker is anxious to re-

move the Knights, for an ending with Rooks will give him
his best drawing chance.

26 . . . .   Kt—Kt4 !

So that if 27 R × P ?, R—
K8 *ch;* 28 K—B2, R × P *ch;*
29 R—Q2 (or 29 K—B3, R—
Kt7), R × R *ch;* 30 K × R, Kt
—B6 *ch* and wins.

27 P—KR4   Kt—K3
28 R—R2   R—K5 ? ?

Weak: the right move was
28 . . . R—B5 ! with decisive advantage. Lasker at once
seizes on the difference:

29 P—B3 !   R—K6
30 R—K2 !

The point; Lasker is able to
extricate himself.

30 . . . .   R—B5
31 R × R   P × R
32 R—Q3   R × RP
33 R × P   Kt—Q5

Threatens 34 . . . R—R8;
35 R—K1, P—KR4 ! ! (but
not 35 . . . Kt × P ?).

34 R—K4

Setting a trap: if 34 . . .

Kt × P ?; 35 R—K8 *ch,* K—
B2; 36 Kt × Kt, R—R8 *ch;* 37
R—K1 and wins.

34 . . . .   R × R
35 P × R   K—B2

Lasker has achieved his objective: the forces are greatly
reduced, so that a draw is very
likely. Yet Nimzovich has the
slight but appreciable advantage of the *outside passed
Pawn.*

36 K—B1   K—B3
37 K—Q2   K—K4

Nimzovich has scored the
first success—a small one but
vital. His King is more aggres-
sively placed, so that White is
continually threatened with a
breakthrough.

38 K—K3   P—KR4

The reader must keep in mind that reduction to a pure Pawn ending always loses for White, for example: 39 Kt—B3 *ch,* Kt × Kt; 40 K × Kt, P —R5; 41 K—Kt4, K × P; 42 K × P, K—Q6 etc.

Nor can White play his Knight to R3: 39 Kt—R3, Kt —B7 *ch;* 40 K—Q2 (40 K— B3, Kt—Kt5; 41 P—R3,* Kt —Q6; 41 P—Kt4, Kt—K8 *ch;* 43 K—K2, Kt—B7 and wins), Kt—Kt5; 41 P—R3, Kt—B3; 42 K—K3, Kt—R4; 43 Kt— B4, Kt—B5 *ch;* 44 K—B3, Kt × KtP; 45 Kt × P, Kt—B5 and wins.

39 P—R3   P—R4
40 Kt—R3   Kt—B7 *ch*
41 K—Q3

After 41 K—Q2 (preventing the Knight from going to K8), Black would play 41 . . . Kt —Q5; 42 K—K3, Kt—K3 and he would soon have the upper hand. In fact, even after the text, Black might have made faster progress with . . . Kt—Q5—K3.

* Later analysis showed that 41 Kt—B4 draws.

41 . . . .   Kt—K8 *ch*
42 K—K2   Kt—Kt7

Giving Lasker a chance to go wrong with 43 K—Q3, Kt —B5 *ch;* 44 Kt × Kt, K × Kt; 45 K—Q4, P—KR5; 46 P— K5, K—B4 *!;* 47 K—Q5, P— R6 and Black queens with check.

43 K—B3   Kt—R5 *ch*
44 K—K3   Kt—Kt3

The Knight has completed an astounding tour. Nimzovich wants to change blockaders, so that his King will be free to threaten an invasion.

45 Kt—Kt5   K—B3
46 Kt—R7 *ch*   K—Kt2
47 Kt—Kt5   K—B3
48 Kt—R7 *ch*   K—K2 *!*

This retreat is very strong. The finesse is that if White's King tries to advance, the exchange of Knights is forced, thus: 49 K—Q4, Kt—B1 *! !* and if 50 Kt—Kt5, Kt—K3 *ch !* again winning with the outside passed Pawn.

49 Kt—Kt5   Kt—K4

At last the blockaders are

reversed! Now Black is ready for action on the Queen-side.

50 K—Q4   K—Q3
51 Kt—R3

After 51 P—Kt3, P—Kt3 White would still have to give way.

51 . . . .   P—QR5 !
52 Kt—B4   P—R5
53 Kt—R3

53 . . . .   P—Kt3 ! !

Still another finesse, and this time a decisive one. If 53 . . . P—Kt4 ?; 54 Kt—B4, Kt—B3 ch; 55 K—B3 !, K—K4; 56 Kt—Kt6 ch. Nimzovich therefore loses a move.

54 Kt—B4   P—Kt4
55 Kt—R3   Kt—B3 ch

And now if 56 K—B3, K—K4 wins in a manner similar to that of the text.

56 K—K3   K—B4
57 K—Q3

Or 57 K—B4, K—Q5; 58 K—B5, Kt—K4; 59 Kt—B2, Kt—B5 and wins. A tense situation!

57 . . . .   P—Kt5 !

Leaving White no choice, for if 58 Kt—B4, P × P; 59 P × P, Kt—K4 ch; 60 K—B2, Kt—B5.

58 P × P ch   K × P

Who would believe that the game is to be decided on the Queen-side after all?!

59 K—B2   Kt—Q5 ch
60 K—Kt1   Kt—K3 !

The key to the win: White's Knight is cut off from Kt5 and B4.

61 K—R2

No better is 61 K—B2, K—B5; 62 Kt—B2, Kt—Kt4 ! (cutting down his colleague's mobility still further) and White is helpless.

61	K—B5
62 K—R3	K—Q5 ! !

Leads to a wonderfully calculated finish.

63 K × P	K × P
64 P—Kt4	K—B6
65 P—Kt5	K—Kt7 ! !

White resigns, for if 66 P—
Kt6 (or 66 Kt—B4 *ch*, Kt ×
Kt; 67 P—Kt6, Kt—K3 !; 68
K—Kt5, Kt—Q1), K × Kt; 67
P—Kt7, Kt—B4 *ch*. A superb
example of the chessmaster's
art. Even Nimzovich rarely
rose to such heights.

58. *Short and Sweet*

NIMZOVICH'S games are rarely short: his subtle style
required a slowly unfolding type of aggression which
became overt only at an advanced stage. There were times,
however, when he unleashed a powerful attack without pre-
liminary maneuver.

Here is such a game. Perhaps his contempt for the Tarrasch Defense spurred him on.

QUEEN'S GAMBIT DECLINED

(in effect)

Stockholm, 1934

WHITE: *A. Nimzovich*   BLACK: *G. Stoltz*

1 P—QB4	P—K3
2 Kt—QB3	P—Q4
3 P—Q4	P—QB4
4 BP × P	KP × P
5 Kt—B3	Kt—QB3

6 P—KKt3	P—B5

The Swedish (or Folkestone)
Defense. Black establishes a
Queen-side majority at the
cost of allowing a White initia-

tive in the center. A lively game is almost always the result.

7 B—Kt2   B—QKt5

8 O—O   KKt—K2
9 P—K4   P × P

Virtually forced; after **9 . . . O—O** a likely continuation is 10 Kt × P, Kt × Kt; 11 P × Kt, Q × P; 12 P—QR3 *!*, B—R4; 13 Kt—K5, Q × P; 14 Kt × Kt, Q × Q; 15 Kt—K7 *ch !* winning a piece.

10 Kt × P   B—KB4 *?*

The Bishop is awkwardly posted here and deprives the Queen Knight Pawn of needed protection. 10 . . . O—O is the best move for equalizing.

11 Kt—K5 *!*   Q × P

The acceptance of the Pawn sacrifice is unfavorable for Black; but 11 . . . Kt × Kt; 12 P × Kt, Kt—B3; 13 Kt —Q6 *ch,* B × Kt; 14 P × B, O—O; 15 B—B4 also leaves White with a fine game.

12 Q × Q   Kt × Q
13 P—QR3 *!*   B × Kt

Or 13 . . . B—R4; 14 Kt —Q6 *ch* and White regains the Pawn and soon wins another one as well.

14 B × B   B—B4
15 B × KtP   QR—Kt1
16 B—QR6   Kt—K7 *ch*
17 K—Kt2

17 . . . .   B—Q5

Stoltz must have intended 17 . . . Kt × B; 18 QR × Kt, R × P; but now he sees that 19 B × P gives White the double threat of 20 B × P *ch* and 20 Kt—Q3.

18 Kt × KBP *!*   Kt × B

Of course if 18 . . . K × Kt; 19 B × P *ch* winning the Knight. The text also proves a frail reed.

19 Kt × R   Kt—Kt6

Stoltz seems to be making progress. Certainly there is no hope in 19 . . . B × KtP; 20 QR × Kt, B × R; 21 R × B etc. Or if 19 . . . Kt—Q6; 20 Kt—B7 *!*

20 QR—Q1   P—Kt3
21 Kt—B7 *!*

Still the same delicious motif!

21 . . . .   K × Kt
22 B × P *ch*   K—B1
23 B × Kt

Removing the Bishop's guard and thus remaining the exchange ahead. The rest is easy.

23 . . . .   B × KtP

24 R—Q3   B × P
25 R—B3 *ch*   K—Kt2

Nimzovich concludes the game now with a neatly executed mating attack.

26 R—QR1   B—B4
27 R—B7 *ch*   K—R3

The mating motif makes its appearance. 28 R—R4 looks attractive, but then 28 . . . Kt —B4 (not 28 . . . R × B *??*; 29 R—R4 *ch,* K—Kt4; 30 P— B4 mate); 29 B—K6, R—Kt7 creates difficulties.

28 R—R5 *!*   B—Kt3

If 28 . . . B—Q3; 29 B— K6 wins easily, or if 28 . . . R × B; 29 R × B and Black can resign. But after the text, Black's Rook will be blocked off from Kt7! Surely a droll variation.

29	R—R4	Kt—B4
30	B—K6	Kt—Q5
31	B—Q7	Resigns

Nimzovich remarks plaintively that his opponent's surrender wards off a pretty Rook sacrifice: 31 . . . R—Kt2; 32 P—Kt4, Kt—Kt6 (if 32 . . . P—Kt4; 33 R—B6 *ch* and 34 R × B); 33 P—Kt5 *ch !*, K × P; 34 R—Kt4 *ch*, K—R3; 35 R—R4 *ch*, K—Kt4; 36 P—B4 *ch !* and mate next move. The game has had witty moments.

index of players

index of openings

(the numbers refer to games)

HOW TO FORCE CHECKMATE
by Fred Reinfeld

If you have difficulty finding the finishing stroke when your opponent is in trouble, then HOW TO FORCE CHECKMATE is designed for you. This is **not** a tedious, scholarly study requiring hours of concentration, a chessboard and pieces, and unlimited time. It **is** a collection of 300 lightning strokes, combinations selected from actual masters' play tournaments, which will form an invaluable background for your own game. Most important of all, they will stimulate your chess instinct so you will be awake to checkmate situations and the best possible way to force the attack.

Either as a concentrated course, or as entertainment for leisure moments, you will find the problems simple to grasp, the diagrams clear (you need no board!), and the solutions easy to understand. New insights into combination, complex or deceptive positions, and ways of estimating the strength and weakness, both of yourself and your opponent, will increase your chess I.Q. and help you win more games.

Starting with one-move checkmates and working up to three mates, you develop the ability to look ahead and plan advance moves. You draw upon the experience and strategy of such masters as Nimzovich, Spielmann, Tarrasch, Capablanca, Morphy, Marshall, Torre, Alekhine, Botvinnik, and others, including modern Russian play, in developing the ability to play the end-game with powerful and decisive strokes. 300 diagrams. Solutions to all positions. 111pp. 5⅜ x 8.

T/// Paperbound **$1.00**

REINFELD ON THE END GAME IN CHESS
by Fred Reinfeld
(Formerly published as PRACTICAL END GAME PLAY)

Written by one of America's foremost chess players and annotators, this excellent popular-level volume analyzes 62 endgames by such masters as Alekhine, Flohr, Tarrasch, Marshall, Morphy, Bogolyubov, Capablanca, Vidmar, Keres, Nimzovich, Rubinstein, Lasker, Reshevsky, and many others.

All games are fully annotated and explained, with extensive quotations from tournament books, collations with similar games, and comments by other experts—all in everyday language you can understand. The author covers such matters as king and pawn endings, minor piece endings, rook and pawn endings, rook and minor piece endings, queen endings, bad bishops, blockage, weak pawns, passed pawns, weak squares, centralization, horizontal maneuvres, and tempo moves.

This book, however, is not primarily concerned with classification of end game situations or with ideal moves. Instead, it centers around transitions from middle play to various types of endplay: favorable endings; unfavorable endings caused by compulsion, or by incorrect choice of move, or disregard of exceptional situations; missed opportunities; and the defence of difficult positions. In each case Mr. Reinfeld points out possible variant moves, material and positional advantages, and general principles of attack and defence.

REINFELD ON THE END GAME IN CHESS is especially valuable for the beginner or intermediate player in its extensive coverage of error. While there are other books which show the narrow range of correct or best play, this is one of the few first-rate books which considers the much larger area of incorrect or weak play. It can aid you immensely by telling you exactly what is wrong with moves you might have made.

62 figures. vi + 177pp. 5⅜ x 8.

Paperbound **$1.25**

LEARN CHESS FROM THE MASTERS

by Fred Reinfeld

(formerly titled CHESS BY YOURSELF)

Improve your chess game, rate your improvement, in the easiest, most instructive way yet devised! Play games against the world's masters: Marshall, Boleslavsky, Znosko-Borovsky, Bronstein, Naidorf, and others.

This volume presents a unique approach: 10 games in which you move against the masters, grade yourself by an easy system provided by Fred Reinfeld, one of the greatest chess expositors and critics. You grade not only for the move that was actually played in tournament, but for optional moves that might have been made.

These 10 games have been specially selected for interest, clarity and easily isolated principles. They illustrate most common, most useful openings, both modern and classical: Queen's Pawn Opening, Ruy Lopez, Dutch Defense, Caro-Kann Defense, Vienna Game, Reti Opening, and French Defense. Full annotations of the highest quality are provided. If you follow through these games carefully, grading yourself for improvement, absorbing the author's easy annotations, you will learn a surprising amount about chess openings in the easiest, most pleasant way.

Ratings and annotations are also provided for 114 extra playing situations that may arise during the game.

91 diagrams. viii + 144pp. 5⅜ x 8.

Paperbound $1.00